Past-into-Present Series

ROADS

Hugh Bodey

Director, Colne Valley Museum

B. T. BATSFORD LTD   London

First published 1971
© Hugh Bodey, 1971

Filmset by Keyspools Ltd, Golborne, Lancashire

Printed in Great Britain by Taylor Garnett Evans & Co. Ltd Radlett
for the Publishers
B. T. Batsford Ltd, 4 Fitzhardinge Street, London W1

7134 1770 6

Acknowledgment

The Author and Publishers wish to thank the following for permission to reproduce the
illustrations included in this book: Aerofilms Ltd for figs. 3, 4, 7, 9, 51, 59, 61; Francis
Armitage for fig. 58; H. A. Bodey for figs. 6, 23, 25, 32, 57; Bristol Corporation for fig.
60; Bristol Museum for fig. 18; Trustees of the British Museum for figs. 12, 13, 19;
British Rail for fig. 50; Colne Valley Museum for fig. 53; Essex County Council for
fig. 30; Herbert Felton for fig. 26; Great Western Railway Museum for fig. 47;
Huddersfield Examiner for fig. 52; John Johnson for figs. 28, 29; John Laing & Son Ltd
for fig. 54; Lancashire Record Office for fig. 43; Leeds City Museum for fig. 24;
National Monuments Record for fig. 11; National Portrait Gallery for fig. 27; H. G.
Pickford & Son for fig. 41; Post Office for fig. 42; Rippon Bros Ltd, Huddersfield, for
fig. 44; Science Museum for figs. 33, 36, 37, 45, 55; Shropshire County Council for
fig. 20; Reece Winstone for figs. 38, 40, 49. The maps were prepared by R. J. Whitaker.

Contents

The Illustrations

1 Prehistoric and Roman Travel

People have always travelled. The earliest settlers in Britain tramped from other parts of Europe when the English Channel was still dry land. They built camps or lived in caves, and roamed around in search of food. Because their wanderings often led the same way each day, simple tracks were formed. These tracks were built for the same purposes as present-day motorways – to take people and goods where they had to go.

Our ancestors abandoned hunting in time, and turned to farming as a more reliable source of food. They built villages of round huts made of stone, wattle, daub and thatch, so that they could live near their fields and animals. Slowly they made contact with neighbouring settlements, and bartered their surplus crop for something else they needed. The forest tracks of the game hunters became instead, defined, grassy paths.

The Bronze Age

These farmers made their settlements in the period of history known as the Bronze Age, which began approximately 2000 B.C. The people were a peaceful race – their largest monument is not a castle but the temple of Stonehenge. People are not afraid to travel when there are no major wars and it seems that the Bronze Age villages traded with each other and, indeed, that merchants came from parts of Europe with their goods. Trade required roads, and the oldest roads still in existence date from this time.

They are known as ridgeways and are mostly to be seen on the chalk and limestone uplands of southern England – Salisbury Plain, the South Downs, the Cotswolds, Mendips, Chilterns and East Anglian Heights.

One of the more important ridgeways began at Beachy Head, Sussex, and passed through Winchester and Old Sarum to Beacon Hill. From there it ran along the top of the Mendips and finished at Bleadon Hill camp, just north of what is now Weston-super-Mare. A ferry service probably continued the route to the Welsh coast somewhere between Cardiff and Barry. Many villages and camps were built near this road, such as Walstonbury camp in Sussex and Old Sarum in Wiltshire, and other structures also, like Chanctonbury Ring in Sussex.

Another important ridgeway was the Icknield Way. This began at Avebury on Salisbury Plain and led the traveller along the Berkshire Downs, Chiltern Hills and East Anglian Heights to the Wash. This was a most important trade route and parts of it form the basis of modern roads, as, for example, the A505 from Dunstable to its junction with the A11, which then continues to follow the way to Thetford,

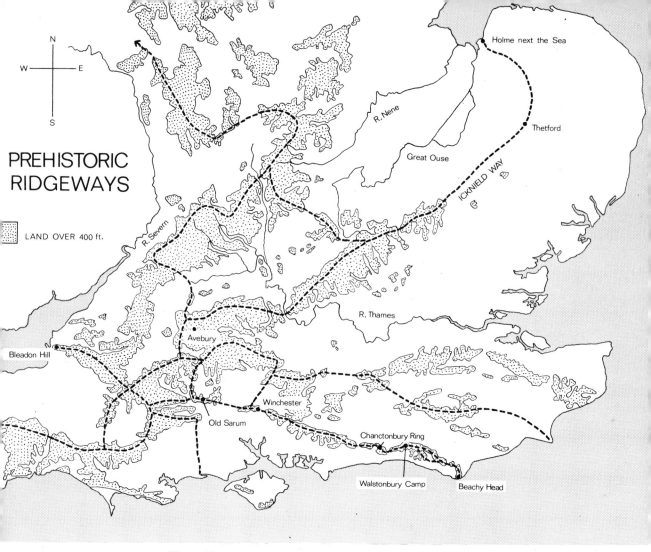

PREHISTORIC RIDGEWAYS

LAND OVER 400 ft.

1 These ridgeways, mostly found in southern England, were the earliest roads, and some are still in existence. The Icknield Way ran from Avebury in Wiltshire to the Wash, while another ridgeway ran from Beachy Head across to Bleadon Hill. There were various branches off these main routes, as the map shows.

Norfolk. Icknield Way turned north from Thetford until it reached the Wash at Holme-next-the-Sea; much of this part is now a footpath, marked on most maps as Peddlers Way.

There were many advantages in having roads along the ridges of the hills. The roads remained dry at all times, so there were no delays from marshes and swollen streams. They were above the forests in the valleys, which made for easier travelling, there was less risk of taking a wrong turning, and there was little chance of an ambush on so open a road as a ridgeway. Nevertheless, the time of greatest danger was after dark, so forts were built ten or twelve miles apart, which was then a day's journey. These forts can usually be found on a hill-top near the road, and have walls and ditches following the contours. Small groups of houses were

6

built near the forts. They now look like chalk pits because they were built a little below ground level, having wattle walls and roofs of sods of earth and bracken. These houses were usually on the sunny side of the hill, and the drinking water was collected in dew ponds at night.

The line of a ridgeway often appears to be marked by conical burial mounds called tumuli. These are frequently in groups, and the arrangement of the groups where roads meet makes them look like signposts. Perhaps Bronze Age people made a memorial to an important person into something that would benefit the living, just as later generations built bridges or wayside fountains.

The Celts

The ridgeways did not fall into disuse when the warlike Iron Age people swept their predecessors aside. There is every sign that the tracks continued to be in constant use, despite the greater danger of travelling. Traders continued to come from afar, and the use of iron bars as currency indicates a considerable local trade. Archaeological excavations at camps like Old Sarum have shown that they were used and adapted by successive waves of invaders, who would also have made use of the adjacent roads. Old Sarum was taken over first by the Iron Age people (the Celts), then in turn by Saxons, Danes and Normans. The roads were used by the Romans, who found them a speedy means of reaching the main Celtic capitals following their invasion of England in A.D. 43. In more recent times the ridgeways were used as ideal routes for driving animals, away from all other traffic, and pack-horses were taken along them within the last hundred years. The constant use of these roads over so long a time has made the grass finer and a darker green than on either side, and this is one guide in following the tracks now.

The Romans

The Romans undoubtedly used the established roads they found but they are better known for building their own roads in very different ways from their predecessors. The Roman invasion of A.D. 43 was a confrontation between two very different types of government. The Romans came from a large empire in which all major matters were decided in Rome and orders dispatched from there to all parts. There had to be a rapid communication system, and the direct route of the roads was designed to allow a galloping horse the best use of its speed. In Britain, by contrast, the Romans found many separate tribes and each village within a tribe was reasonably independent. The ridgeways had been used for trade, and followed the line of the hills, which was seldom the most direct way. The side tracks were faint and rambling, particularly north and west of the midlands. There had to be a new pattern of roads superimposed on the old if the Roman generals hoped to conquer the whole of Britain and to govern it later.

That is why the Roman roads were as straight as possible, often overriding obstacles that other road-builders would have avoided. Speedy travel for galloping horses and marching legions was the only reason for the early Roman roads, and

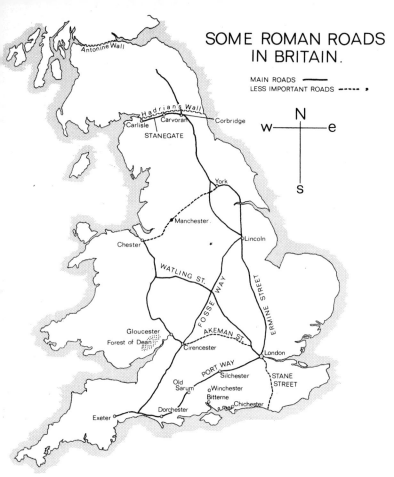

SOME ROMAN ROADS
IN BRITAIN.

MAIN ROADS ———
LESS IMPORTANT ROADS ----- ▸

2 It is not difficult to see from this map how the Romans acquired their reputation for straight roads. All their roads radiated from London, but although they were useful for transporting troops, they tended to by-pass important regional trading centres.

all other considerations were secondary. The 5,000 miles of roads were not all built at once but they were all planned at the start. The main roads and many lesser ones were built between A.D. 43 and 81, which was the period of most rapid conquest.

All the main roads radiated from London, the capital of this Roman province, and led to the legionary fortress towns, such as York, Chester and Gloucester. This made it possible to send orders and reinforcements of troops, and made the work of government easier. The roads were also helpful to civilians wishing to travel the same way. These roads did not benefit most of the local traffic, however, for they frequently by-passed the more populous areas, like the Cotswolds, instead of running through them. There are signs, too, that even government officials found the roads a little too direct, ignoring tribal capitals that did not lie in the path of the road. The official who compiled the routes in a road-book of the third century called the *Antonine Itinerary* ignored the Roman Stane Street across the uninhabited Weald when describing the way between London and Chichester. Instead he described a route through the towns of Silchester and Winchester and the port of Bitterne, which was twice as long as Stane Street but took a traveller where people lived. Later, in the third and fourth centuries, more local roads were built, all to carry trade.

3 Stane Street across the Weald of Sussex is a good example of a Roman road. It was built to take iron and grain to London in the shortest possible time. Like the other roads over the Weald, it ignored villages that could have been linked together.

Construction of Roman Roads

The first stage in building a road was to plan its route. This was done by skilled engineers serving with the army. They had neither maps nor compasses to guide them, and England was largely forested. It was therefore a considerable achievement for the Romans to route the roads so accurately over long distances. The next stage was marking out the road on the ground. This was done from one hill to the next. Gangs of men manoeuvred beacon fires until all could be seen in a straight line. This produced the best known characteristic of a Roman road, its straightness, as can be seen, for example, in a four-mile stretch of King Street, between Sandbach and Warrington in Cheshire (parts of A530 and B5309).

There are some bends in Roman roads, however, and these can mostly be seen on the tops of hills, between one straight stretch and the next. The engineers did not attempt the impossible. Their planning avoided the major obstacles, and they constructed a winding road if it was useful to follow a ridge or valley. A steep valley was negotiated with a terraced road following the curves of the valley side or even by zig-zags, until a straight route could be resumed. A road was taken up the bank of a river at times to find a shallow part where slabs could be laid for a ford, then it doubled back to continue from where the route was broken. Roman engineers could also bridge rivers, as they did with a fine wooden structure at Chesters in Northumberland, but these were costly to build and maintain, and only used where the amount of traffic justified it. If you set out to trace a Roman road today you will mostly find long straight stretches, but you may also find bends near rivers and in hilly districts. The gradient of hill that the troops took in their stride may surprise you.

4 This bridge at Castle Combe in Wiltshire was built by the Romans, though the parapet wall is not their work. The bridge replaced a ford that frequently flooded.

Once the route had been marked out troops and defeated British slaves started on the construction. The roads fall into two classes, main roads and minor roads; an example of a main road is the Port Way between Silchester and Old Sarum. There were two groups within the main road category, those sixty-two feet wide between the ditches and the more important ones which were eighty-four feet wide. The Port Way was one of the latter, being part of the road linking London and Exeter. It will be seen from the cross-section (fig. 5) that the actual road is twenty-four feet wide, which is the average width for main roads, and that it is raised above ground level.

This embankment is also a feature of the main roads and is called an agger. It reaches a height of seventeen inches in this part of the Port Way but can vary from a few inches on some roads to five feet on parts of Ermine Street. The surface soil was cleared from the site before the agger was built on the subsoil out of local materials. In this case the base layer was of chalk rammed down hard and cambered (i.e. sloped up from the edges to the middle of the road) up to seven inches. Then a four-inch layer of flints was laid by hand and a sprinkling of chalk used to fill any gaps. A final layer of local gravel was laid with a camber of six inches, making a road that men and wagons could travel with ease. A 30-feet space was cleared on each side of the agger and was intended for animals and other slow-moving traffic. These sections sloped away to the ditches, completing the drainage system. Such roads allowed troops to march at thirty miles a day to trouble-spots and it is quite possible that the size and precision of the roads, a symbol of Roman efficiency, was enough to strike terror into some of the Britons.

The minor roads were narrower, averaging fifteen to eighteen feet, and had no cleared spaces or drainage ditches. The road was sometimes properly built and on an agger, but more often was laid directly on to the subsoil. The materials used were never carried more than a few miles, so there are many variations. Gravel was preferred, being ready for use and easy to lay. Broken flint was also used, and other types of rock broken and used. Iron slag was used on the Dean road in Gloucestershire, which rusted into a hard-wearing surface. Roads were only paved with flat slabs or cobbles in towns or near the banks of a river.

The cross-section is of part of Stanegate near Chesterholm, Northumberland. Stanegate ran between Corbridge and Carvoran to the south of Hadrian's Wall. The road was just fifteen feet wide and only a few inches above ground level. The surface soil was removed, and heavy stones from six to twelve inches square

5 On the Port Way, the road itself, raised above the embankment (the agger) is 24 feet wide. On either side is a 30-foot space cleared for slow-moving traffic. Stanegate, however, a minor road, was narrower, with no cleared spaces or drainage ditches.

THE CONSTRUCTION OF ROMAN ROADS.

1. PORT WAY : A MAIN ROAD
RUNNING FROM SILCHESTER TO OLD SARUM. DISTANCE 36 MILES.

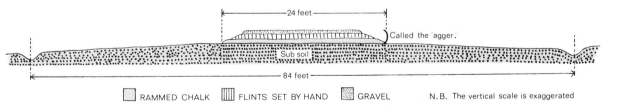

— 24 feet —

Called the 'agger.'

Sub soil

— 84 feet —

☐ RAMMED CHALK ⫿⫿⫿ FLINTS SET BY HAND ⸭ GRAVEL   N.B. The vertical scale is exaggerated

2. STANEGATE : A MINOR ROAD
RUNNING FROM CORBRIDGE TO CARVORAN. DISTANCE 21 MILES.

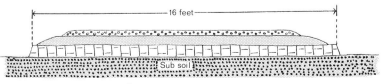

— 16 feet —

Sub soil

⊞ HEAVY STONES ☐ CLAY OR TURF BEDDING ⸭ PEBBLES OR 2inch SANDSTONES
Vertical scale greatly exaggerated

carefully laid as a foundation. The layer of clay and turf served as a bedding for the two-inch layer of sandstone pebbles which made the surface. Part of Stanegate had to be built on terraces as it descended steep valley sides near Corbridge. The cambers on minor roads were often steep, and in extreme cases the edges were twelve inches below the centre on a width of only fifteen feet.

Roman traffic

The whole network of main roads was constructed during the rapid military advance between A.D. 43 and 81. This coincided with a time when roads throughout the Roman Empire were being built for the swift passage of troops and government officials, and for the slower movement of army supplies and goods paid as tribute by conquered tribes. Most goods were moved by pack animal, so that steep hills were no real obstacle. Slow, four-wheeled wagons were also used, and the faster, two-wheeled chariot carried standing passengers. The fastest way of travelling, however, was on horseback (and that was not surpassed until 1830). Bulky and breakable goods went by river and sea wherever possible.

Roads were built to help trade from the second century onwards. These may well have been planned by ex-army engineers, though they were mainly narrow and had shorter straight lengths. Many such roads were built across the Weald to allow the Sussex corn and iron to be taken to London. Another example is the road through the Forest of Dean in Gloucestershire, which went from Weston-under-Penyard to the harbour at Lydney, where it also joined the coast road from Gloucester to Caerleon. The principal traffic again was iron, and also timber and food. A more impressive road is a stretch of more than a mile on the Yorkshire Moors, known as Wade's Causeway. The purpose of this road is unknown.

The Dark Ages

The last of the legions was recalled to Rome in 410. Roman ways were followed until about 450, but the scattered invasions by Picts in the north and Saxons in the south-east gradually broke up the unified way in which Britain had been governed. The roads were no longer needed by government officials, and traders only travelled short distances for local journeys. Road maintenance ceased, and slowly the roads were allowed to decay. Wooden bridges rotted and fell away, wash-outs were caused by flooded streams, trees fell and blocked the way, and tree roots broke up the foundations. The Saxons had no use for town markets and therefore did not need the roads that led there. Some parts of the roads became overgrown and impassable, others turned into marshy, hollow ways. The one use the Saxons did find for them was as boundaries between fields and, later, between parishes. The roads were still sufficiently obvious to be landmarks. The gradual decay explains how nowadays you can travel along a straight road that is clearly built over or alongside its Roman counterpart, but then swings sharply away where, long ago, part of the Roman way became impassable.

The long series of Saxon raids, and the Viking invasions that followed, brought

6 Part of the road through the Forest of Dean, Gloucestershire, built to take iron goods from Mitcheldean to Lydney harbour. The surface gravel has washed away, showing the heavy foundation blocks and kerb stones. The road is eight feet wide, and this section at Blackpool Bridge is always on view.

7 Ryknield Way, Warwickshire, is a more typical Roman road. The direction changes at the top of the hill where the engineers could look over the valley beyond. The road down the very steep hill in the foreground (marked by the line of trees) has been abandoned so that wheeled vehicles could take the gentler slope to the right·

troubled times to Britain. The country again became a number of kingdoms within one island, towns were abandoned as people moved nearer to forts and hill-top castles. Trade declined and there was less need for roads. Many years passed before this situation changed.

In the tenth and eleventh centuries, when England again became united under one king, trade began to increase and roads again had some importance. A variety of tracks were used – parts of the Roman roads and of the older ridgeways, and also new paths which often followed field edges. It became the common custom that each parish was responsible for the roads that passed through it. The rule was rarely enforced but became the pattern for road maintenance in later centuries.

Case Study

The last section of each chapter in this book describes the many roads that have been used by travellers between Leeds and Manchester, concentrating on those that have gone through or near the Colne Valley in Yorkshire. This valley and the hills on each side of it have been used for centuries, so their history illustrates some of the general history of roads made earlier in the chapter. There are some local differences, as you will find if you start enquiring about the roads near you.

8 The map clearly shows examples of the various roads available to medieval travellers in the Huddersfield area. Both the ridgeway and the Roman road kept to the sides of the valley, the former being taken north from Delph to avoid peat moors before running in a straight line to the fort at Slack.

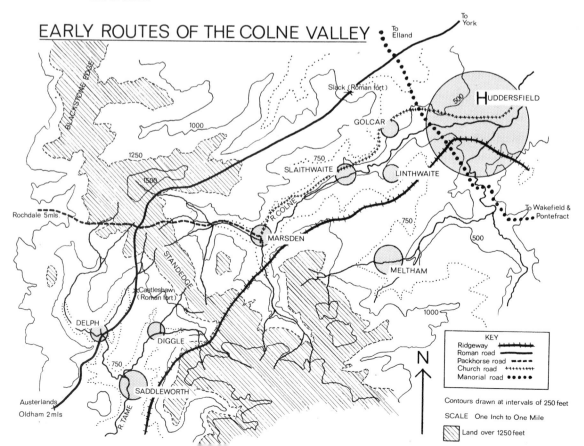

9 The road over Blackstone Edge in Yorkshire is very steep. The surface is paved with stone, which the Romans seldom did outside towns. The groove down the middle of the road is thought to have been worn by poles which were trailed behind carts to act as a brake

The Colne Valley comes within three miles of the Tame Valley, so it became obvious for roads to take advantage of this when they were built in the bottoms of valleys. Before that the roads kept to the high ground on each side of the valley, which is free of large areas of marsh and has several gaps in the otherwise steep escarpments facing Lancashire. It was a natural route, and became more useful with the gradual growth of Manchester and Leeds. Most attention is paid in these chapters to the Colne Valley section of the roads because they have been kept close to each other and this makes for a clearer account in so short a space.

The earliest road was a ridgeway that ran along the southern side of the valley. It could not always be on the highest land because of peat marshes, but it never came lower than 200 feet above the forests and swamps in the valley. Once over the summit, the road went due south, using the steep eastern side of the Tame valley. The ridgeway can no longer be followed in the Colne Valley (see Chapter 3) but Bronze Age traders used this road as part of the route between the east and west coasts. It was still being used by the Celts centuries later when the capital of the powerful Brigantes tribe was in the Huddersfield area. Traders came here from as far away as Italy about the year A.D. 20, as well as from other parts of Britain.

The Roman engineers had other ideas. They planned a new road on the north side of the river. This road, built in 79–80, was a link between the legionary capitals of Chester and York, and passed through Manchester. The nine miles from Manchester to Austerlands was one straight length, and wherever possible the rest of the road was built to the same high standard. From Austerlands the road followed the curve of the hillside to Delph, part of it being built on a terrace, and then it became straight to the first fort at Castleshaw. The road was then taken north to avoid peat moors before resuming the north-east direction of most of the road. The rest of the road ran in long straight lengths to the next fort at Slack, and the modern A640 to Slack and A643 to Brighouse run beside the Roman road for much of the way. The two forts were abandoned about the year 130 and the more northerly route over the paved road at Blackstone Edge was used instead. Both roads used the most direct route and, like the ridgeways, kept aloof from the obstacles in the river valleys.

2 Trade and Travel

The Middle Ages

The coming of the Normans in 1066 brought no immediate changes to the roads. Trade continued to be largely a local business, while government officials such as those who carried out the Domesday survey in 1086 travelled on horseback. Trade began to increase in the twelfth century, and the volume of traffic with it. Most of the Roman roads were still serviceable despite centuries of neglect. Three of these roads, Watling Street, Ermine Street and Foss Way, together with the prehistoric Icknield Way, were regarded as royal roads. Travellers on them were under the king's protection – anyone attacking them could be fined 100 shillings. The roads had to be wide enough for two wagons to pass or for sixteen armed knights to ride abreast. A tax called pavage was collected at times to maintain the surface of these roads. Gradually the idea of some roads being the king's highway was extended to other well-used roads as the volume of traffic grew. The idea was repeated in the Great Charter sealed by John in 1215, where he promised that, 'All merchants shall have safe conduct to go and come out of and into England, and to stay in and travel through England by land and water for purchase or sale . . . except in time of war. . . '.

These roads must not be judged by twentieth-century standards, however. The safe conduct was to protect the lives and property of the king's servants and other travellers, who were regarded with suspicion and hostility in places distant from London. The first law about roads was the Statute of Winchester, passed in 1285. This tried to end the threat of ambush by ordering the removal of all dykes, bushes and woods for 200 feet on either side of the road. The roads were not intended for rapid long-distance travel but for slow ox-carts and pack-trains travelling to the hundreds of fairs and markets in England. Some idea of the number of these can be gained by looking up the number of place-names with 'market' or 'chipping' (which means market) in them, such as Market Drayton, Shropshire, and Chipping Camden, Gloucestershire.

If the main roads were not good, the other roads were both bad and unsafe. They were meandering cart-tracks, on which the king guaranteed nothing. Frequent obstructions and delays were encountered, such as flooded streams making fords impassable and ferries hazardous, or fallen trees or dumped rubbish. Many of these obstacles were also found on the highways but there was a way round them – a 'highway' was not just a track but the right of the king and his people to go that way. If the road were impassable, travellers were within their rights to take to the fields, regardless of fences and crops. Landowners who disliked that idea had to ensure that there was free passage on the road adjoining their land.

10 The bridge at Newcastle-on-Tyne was built in the Middle Ages. The fortified stone gateway is on the north end of the bridge. Bridges were popular sites for houses (built out on wooden supports) where the air was fresher. A great flood did the damage in 1771.

Some improvements were made from the end of the twelfth century onwards. Bridges were built, and existing wooden bridges rebuilt of stone. London Bridge was built in 1176, and lasted until a flood in 1206, and the stone bridge at Huntingdon was built in 1300. Bridges were expensive to build and the money came from many sources. London Bridge and also the old Newcastle Bridge had houses built on them, and rents paid by the tenants helped to maintain the bridges. Some bridges were built as part of a town's defences, such as the heavily-fortified Monnow bridge in Monmouth. Most bridges, however, were paid for by private gifts, which were encouraged and often added to by the Church. Some bridges, as in Wakefield and Rotherham, still have chapels built into them as a result. Merchants contributed by the end of the Middle Ages, since they had much to gain from being able to cross without hindrance. The stone bridge at Bideford, Devon, was erected about 1460, largely out of the wealth of local wool merchants, and the builders used the previous wooden bridge as scaffolding.

Travellers and Vehicles

Most medieval travellers went on foot and most goods were carried by animals. Poor people walked, whether to market or on a pilgrimage; only the wealthy could afford to go on horseback. There were few vehicles to choose from, and they were rarely seen on the roads far from London.

A hammock-wagon was available for the elderly in the eleventh century. Two centuries later, King John's last campaign made use of most ways of travel, and met with many of the hazards. John travelled on horse-back from Wales to Norfolk, in 1216 covering between thirty and fifty miles a day. In October, he and his army marched from Kings Lynn to Swineshead, Lincolnshire, by the safe but roundabout road through Wisbech, so avoiding the quicksands of the Wash.

17

11 Huntingdon Bridge, an important and graceful structure. It was built about 1300. It looks as if two different architects built it, their designs meeting in the middle.

The carts and pack-horses, carrying a mountain of stores, treasure, clothing and equipment, attempted the direct but dangerous route across the four-mile estuary of the Wellstream. Although they started at low tide and with a local guide, the whole convoy sank into the sand as the tide rose. John continued his journey to Newark but caught a fever and had to be carried in a litter – a bed with roof and curtains, carried on poles by two horses in single file.

Coaches appeared in the fourteenth century and a canvas-covered wagon called a whirlicote was used by ladies and invalids. Many ladies preferred to ride side-saddle on a horse than be jolted in an unsprung carriage. Horse-litters were still being used on ceremonial occasions in the sixteenth century: the one that took both Catherine of Aragon and Anne Boleyn to their weddings had the poles covered in crimson velvet, pillows and cushions of white satin and an awning of cloth of gold.

Food and other goods mostly went on the backs of pack-animals, though carts were available. The cost of carriage by cart remained constant from 1260 to 1540, at a penny a mile for a ton of grain and double for heavy loads like lead and tiles. Carts were sometimes used over long distances in the fourteenth century, so the roads must have been adequate for the amount of traffic then; merchants began to complain early in the sixteenth century that the roads were no longer adequate.

The kinds of traveller changed markedly between 1350 and 1540. Pilgrims, monks, friars and people going to fairs made up most of the travellers about 1350; by 1540 the monasteries were closed, many of the fairs had ceased and few pilgrims visited the holy shrines. Instead traders, merchants and their goods made up most of the mobile population. This led to an enlarged pattern of main roads, a change evident by 1500. The old main roads radiating from London were still important because London was cut off from all the country's rivers except the Thames and only roads could link the capital with the midlands. In addition, roads in the north and west, linking the country's important towns were in frequent use, such as the road from Bristol through Gloucester to Chester. These were not built as new roads but were simply older, busier routes. (New roads were rarely constructed, and then only for military purposes, such as a road built by Henry I over Wenlock Edge, Shropshire, in 1102.)

The monasteries had played an active part in maintaining the roads, both by their own efforts and by encouraging others to help. Many bridges were built by them. No one took over their work, however, when the monasteries were closed by Act of Parliament in the 1530s. Henry VIII took the lands and buildings as his own but did not take over the task of maintaining the roads. This was left to individuals and to the parishes but little effort was made to see that any repairs were done. Yet the volume of traffic continued to increase as the woollen and other industries exported more.

Some individuals tried to find remedies. An Act of 1523 allowed the owner of the manor of Hempstead in Kent to enclose an old road and make a new one. Parliament took the opportunity to allow other landowners to do the same, since

12 The oldest drawing of an English vehicle is this hammock wagon, taken from an eleventh-century manuscript. There were no springs or brakes, and no shelter from the weather. It was probably only used for invalids (an ambulance) and then only in or near the towns.

13 A dog-cart needing a helping hand over uneven ground, drawn in the fourteenth century. The vehicle is little more than a box. The nails protruding from the wheels helped to stop the cart slipping in thick mud. The leading dog seems to be doing all the work!

'many other common ways in the said County of Kent be so steep and noyous by wearing and course of water . . . that people cannot have their carriages or passages by horses upon . . . the same, but to their great pains, peril and jeopardy'. There was no compulsion in that Act, but there was in the Statute of Bridges, passed in 1531. This was concerned with the repair of bridges and laid down that, unless a local custom held that some particular person or organisation was responsible, town bridges were to be maintained by the local citizens, while all others were to be kept up by the Justices of the Peace of the county, who could levy a rate at the quarter-sessions if necessary.

Highways Act 1555

Laying the responsibility on ratepayers and citizens was taken a stage further in the Highways Act of 1555, which became the basis for road maintenance even down to the nineteenth century. This revived the almost-forgotten Saxon idea that each parish should be responsible for the roads passing through it. The parishioners were to elect a Surveyor of Highways annually and, under his direction, were to work for four days a year (six days from 1563) on repairing the roads. This work became known as statute labour. Everyone with land valued at £50 per year had to send a cart with two men to bring stone, while farmers had to provide a man and a horse.

The parish had long been held responsible for its own roads but there had never been any way of enforcing the law. The new Act provided enforcements. The idea of having a surveyor of highways was new, and he was presented with a daunting list of duties. He had to take over the accounts as soon as he was elected, find out where the money came from to repair the roads, examine the roads and bridges in the parish three times a year, persuade owners of land adjoining a road to clear away any rubbish or overhanging trees and clear the drains, stop any vehicles that did not comply with the law, and, of course, organise the annual week of repairs. The job was unpaid, and a person could be fined £5 if he refused to take it on.

The Act also ordered the Justices of the Peace to inspect the roads in their county from time to time. A parish that neglected its duty to repair the roads could be indicted, that is the surveyor or a J.P. could accuse the whole parish at the quarter-sessions of breaking the law. If the parish were found guilty a heavy fine was imposed; three months were allowed for payment, but the fine was not collected if the roads were repaired in that time. The surveyor of Derbyshire attended the county court in 1658 and presented 'the inhabitants of Duffield for not repairing Cowhouse Lane being in the said parish, and in great decay, and ought by them to be repaired being used for all carts and carriages.' In effect the parish was accused of neglect.

Presentment had advantages in road repair. It was a way round the poor results produced by statute labour, it made available more money than the sixpenny rate that a surveyor could collect by that time, and it concentrated attention on bad stretches of road. On the other hand, it was a costly way of raising money and did not guarantee a good road. The surveyor was still the man in charge of the work, and he only had to make the surface as good as before – not even the courts could compel a better standard of road, however much the increased traffic demanded it.

The 1555 Act thus gave the surveyor an arduous year in office. Although he, the Justices, and owners of land alongside a road, all had responsibilities, the ultimate duty to keep the roads in a passable state rested on the whole parish. Statute labour and highway rates fell on them all, and, if they did not carry out the surveyor's wishes, the court's fine had to be paid by them all too.

All the arrangements in the Act looked splendid on paper, and must have served some purpose because they were renewed every seven years until 1586, and then made permanent. It would be a mistake, however, to think that the law was followed to the letter in every parish or that the roads became magnificent. The first weakness of the law was the surveyor. Doctors and clergymen were excused election and the gentry were not interested. Yet these were the very people who travelled and knew what roads in other areas were like. Instead, the surveyor was elected from among the farmers, craftsmen and innkeepers, men who could seldom travel far and who were too busy to take on any new work and do it well. There was little hope of any good ideas from them.

The money they needed for stone and other new works could only come from a rate, and all surveyors knew how unpopular that would be because they had all grumbled about it when other surveyors tried to raise money. This left the surveyor with what he could make out of statute labour and the fines on people who refused to work. (This refusal became increasingly common in the seventeenth century in some parishes. In 1670 the fines were fixed at one shilling and sixpence a day for a labourer, three shillings for a man with a horse and ten shillings for a cart, animals and two men.)

Another trouble was that the surveyor could not be everywhere at once, so that while he was superintending work in one part of the parish, the men were standing idle everywhere else. In a book written between 1557 and 1587 William Harrison wrote that, '. . . the rich do so cancel their portions [i.e. statute labour] and the poor so loiter in their labours, that of all the six, scarce two good day's work are performed . . .'. Probably the system could never have worked, quite apart from human failings, because the surveyor could only have employed all the men usefully if the materials were ready on the first day of the week set aside for repairs. This was impossible since he could not summon work at any other time than the one week. Therefore many men would have to wait while stones were being fetched before they could start work.

The surveyors were never chosen for their knowledge of road mending, and most were content if they opened up the roads across the commons after the winter and heaped earth over the deeper ruts. Some parishes kept a road plough (normally housed in the churchyard) and this they used in the spring, since most travellers avoided the winter months. The edges were thrown up into a furrow in the centre of the road, and this was flattened with a harrow for summer traffic. Soft dirt-roads patched with stones picked off the fields covered most of Britain in the sixteenth century and well into the nineteenth century. (More is said about parish maintenance of the roads in chapters 3, 4 and 5.)

The system suited Parliament and farmers alike and so it was kept, despite its wastefulness and futility. Certain it is that the roads were dreadful in 1600 and became worse – little maintenance work was done during the Civil War. The Commonwealth Parliament of 1654 allowed parishes to collect an annual highway rate, and this worked wonders where it was collected and used wisely. The rate was abolished, however, in 1660.

Maps and Vehicles

Parliament had done its best for the roads by the 1555 Act and its subsequent amendments; attention was also turned to the vehicles that used the roads. Nearly all the legislation was aimed at preventing the roads from becoming any worse through excessive wear. The volume of traffic had been increasing steadily from the end of the fifteenth century, and had led to regular services being operated by carriers' wagons. Carts ran between Ipswich and London three times a week in 1599. John Taylor published a book called *Carriers Cosmography* in 1637, which gives information of an organised goods traffic at that time. Men caught up in the Civil War visited new parts of the country with the armies, and expected improved travel facilities after the war.

14 This drawing of a coach was made in 1690. It is heavy and cumbersome, and does not seem to have any springs. Six horses are needed to draw it, even on a level road, which looks rough and stony.

The demand was met in two ways. One was in the supply of maps. This started with the series of county maps drawn by Christopher Saxton in the 1570s, which showed every town, village and country house, every port, river and stream, but no roads. *An Intended Guide for English Travellers*, first published in 1625 by John Nordern, gave the distances by road between main towns. This book went through many editions. Oliver Cromwell ordered a map of England to be made in 1644. It was produced by Wenceslaus Hollar, who included the main roads in the country, and remained in use until John Ogilby's more accurate maps appeared in 1675.

The other way in which the demand for better transport facilities was met was by an increasing variety of vehicles. Walter Rippon built a coach for the Earl of Rutland in 1555, which is thought to have been the first of a new continental style built in England. Most nobles and gentlemen had their coaches by 1600. Elizabeth I had two; one of them was built by Walter Rippon in 1564, but she had so painful a journey in it the first time that she never used it again. She preferred to go by horse, or in a litter on ceremonial occasions. Although the carriage at this time was a cumbersome vehicle, it was also fragile and lacking springs. Thomas Platter travelled in one from London to Oxford, but his coachman refused to go on to Cambridge partly because one wheel was damaged and partly because 'the road was too boggy and difficult to find, for that neighbourhood was uninhabited and rather deserted'.

Parliament tried to restrict the number of coaches in 1601 for fear that there would not be enough horses for the army, but the ban failed. Fynes Moryson noted in 1615 that 'the streets of London are almost stopped up with them': there were estimated to be 6,000 coaches in the city in 1634. The hackney coach was available for hire in London in 1625, where the standard of driving soon had them called Hackney Hell Carts! Sedan chairs were popular with the ladies in the 1630s. The watermen who ran the Thames ferries complained at these intruders on their trade, and persuaded Parliament to limit the number of hackney carriages to fifty in 1637. This was increased to 300 in 1654 and to 400 in 1662. There was more than enough trade for coaches, sedan chairs and ferries, for London was expanding at this time and many of its inhabitants becoming wealthier.

Stage coaches were operating from London by 1650. These ran at set times and stopped at recognised stages, which were usually roadside inns, where food for the passengers and fresh horses were available. The charge was one shilling for five miles. Three main routes from London had three stage coaches a week in 1658, to Exeter and Plymouth, to Chester and Kendal, and to Wakefield, York and Newcastle. The journey from London to Exeter took four days and cost £2. The passengers had a seat in a springless coach and had to travel from five in the morning until nine at night. Coach sickness was all too common. The fortnightly stage to Edinburgh cost £4 for a single journey. The range of routes multiplied after 1660, due to increased demand for passenger travel. A flying coach service was started in 1669 between Oxford and London, making the journey in thirteen hours, which was an average of just over four miles an hour.

The royal posts went by horseback and were therefore much faster. In Elizabeth's reign there were five post roads from London – to Dover for ambassadors in Europe, to Berwick and Carlisle, to Cornwall, to north Wales and to south Wales. These routes were also divided into stages where fresh horses were kept solely for the mails and for people carrying the Queen's orders. The system was extended in 1635 with by-posts operating from stages along the minor roads. Other people could send letters if they could afford the charges, which ranged from twopence for a letter within a radius of eighty miles from London to eightpence if addressed to Scotland.

The volume of goods being moved also increased, much of it by the traditional pack animals. Bales of cloth were sent from Exeter to London at the end of the seventeenth century by pack-horse. The horses were roped together into strings – up to nine horses to a string were allowed by law – and usually several strings travelled together. The animals left Exeter every Saturday, travelled about twenty-five miles a day, and arrived in London the following Friday. The Roman road was used as far as Honiton, and was still the best stretch of road on this route, despite its age.

Limits on the Use of Roads

The main victims of Parliamentary pressure were people moving goods by cart. Proclamations were issued in 1621 and 1629 banning loads over one ton from the roads, but they were ineffectual. A Highways Act in 1662 limited the number of horses to a maximum of seven to haul one load, and ordered a minimum width of four inches for cart wheels. County courts acted in a similar way: the Kent justices complained in 1604 that whereas carts seldom used to haul more than a ton, now two-and-a-half tons had become common. As a result, 'the highway from Canterbury to Sittingbourne is thereby spoiled to the great annoyance of all travellers', and the owners of carts carrying more than one ton were made to pay five shillings towards mending the road. Both courts and government were struggling to keep the existing system in repair. Few men could see that, instead of attempting a Canute on the rising tide of traffic, it would be more helpful to assist with the building of new roads and bridges. Trade continued to increase after 1660 and the policy of conserving existing roads was ruined as effectively as the road surfaces.

Case Study

The old roads were still in use north and south of the Colne in the Middle Ages. The accounts of the honour of Clitheroe between 1296 and 1305 show frequent traffic using the Bronze Age tracks through the valley and over the Pennines, while in 1291 Hugh of Elland was given the right to take tolls from any person taking goods over the Blackstone Edge road. The tolls were to be spent on repairing the road for the benefit of travellers.

Other roads were developed in the area during the Middle Ages, serving quite different needs. The Colne Valley came under the manor of Wakefield soon after the Norman Conquest, and a track was formed by the many people who went there on official business. The two parish churches for the Valley were at Almondbury for the south bank and Huddersfield for the north. New roads were made by people going to church, and these roads were lower than the ridgeways but still not in the bottom of the valley. Fountains Abbey owned moorland in the area, and used some of its wealth to build bridges over the Colne and the Calder to aid travellers going between Manchester and Leeds. None of these roads, however, would have been any use to wheeled vehicles. Instead, most of the people went on foot and the goods were carried by people or pack-animals. Many generations passed before a cart was seen in the Colne Valley.

3 The Early Turnpikes, 1660–1770

Increased traffic and early improvements

The restoration of Charles II in 1660 brought settled times to England. This encouraged people to travel and merchants to trade over a wider area than they had for many years. It soon became more obvious than ever that the trade by which Britain lived depended on the transport of goods. London and the larger provincial towns such as Bristol, Norwich and Coventry needed regular supplies of food from outlying areas, and the main industries of cloth-making and the metal trades needed raw materials and ways of sending their goods to the ports. Britain was still a large number of self-contained regions but these regions were increasingly having to trade with each other and with the outside world.

This trade required roads, and also rivers and ports. Most bulky goods were sent by river and the sea for as much of their journey as possible. The coal trade from Newcastle to London was an example of this. It was frequently necessary to use roads to take goods to the river, or from the river to the customer. It cost four times as much to take cloth twenty-five miles by land from Leeds to York as to send it fifty miles from York to Hull on the river Ouse. The roads were links in a transport system centred on rivers and the sea for all heavy goods.

Other kinds of goods, however, did travel by land. The roads in the east midlands and south-east were made worse by the constant traffic towards London. Most of the city's meat walked to London, at least until the 1730s, and the army of hooves churned up the clay and dust. Every year 40,000 Highland cattle were herded from Scotland to be fattened in Norfolk, and then continued into London. Thirty thousand black cattle walked from Wales to the south-east England pastures, and finished their journey in Smithfield market. Geese and chickens, pigs and sheep, were all shepherded towards London's growing population. Relays of horses even carried fish to London, fresh from the boats in Lyme Regis. Animals walking to market were not peculiar to London – a smaller version of this animal army was marched into the markets and fairs of all the market towns, and other farm produce was also taken there. Part of an old nursery rhyme, probably first sung in the eighteenth century, tells of this kind of traffic seen on the roads:

> *As I was going to Banbury,*
> *Upon a summer's day,*
> *My dame had butter, eggs and fruit,*
> *And I had corn and hay;*
> *Joe drove the ox, and Tom the swine,*
> *Dick took the foal and mare...*

The animals walked. The 'dame' carried the groceries in baskets, perhaps hung from a yoke across her shoulders. Only the corn and hay would have needed some kind of cart, such as a hay-wain.

Charles II realised the urgent need of better roads. As a first step he requested John Ogilby to survey all the main roads and his maps were published in 1675 as a book called *Britannia*. These were the first road maps to be based on accurate surveys. The King's interest reflected the opinion of merchants and others that many improvements were urgently needed. Transport mattered to a trading country.

Parliament also tried to help. An Act passed in 1691 urged that all main roads should be widened to eight feet but little notice was taken of that. An Act of 1698 authorised the Justices to erect guide posts at main cross-roads to indicate where these roads led. This law was acted on, and it was extended in the 1730s to include guide stones on moors and commons, giving distances to neighbouring villages.

15　John Ogilby and his assistants spent many months measuring and mapping main roads, and their work was published in 1675. The roads are drawn in strips, each with its own compass showing how they fit together. Some indication is given as to what the traveller will see from the road.

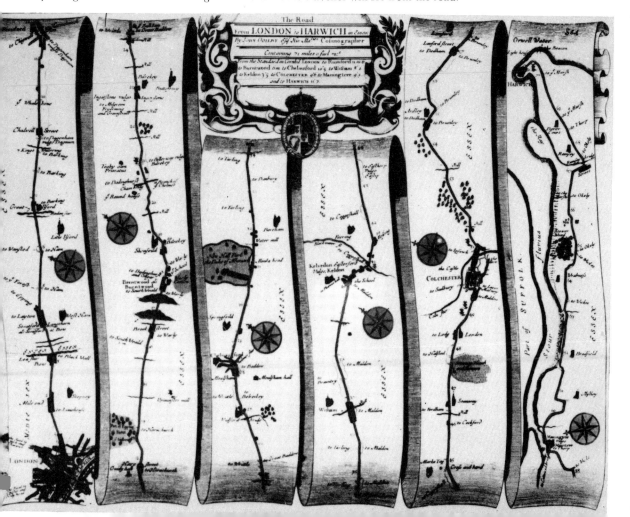

The spirit of improvement even touched the surface of short lengths of a few roads. One or two post-roads were made a little smoother and in 1663 the Justices in Hertfordshire, Cambridgeshire and Huntingdonshire were given the necessary legal powers to collect tolls from travellers on the Great North Road and to use the money to repair the road. Toll gates were to be set up at Wadesmill in Hertfordshire, at Caxton in Cambridgeshire and at Stilton in Huntingdonshire. Only the first of these raised enough money for adequate repairs to be made. (The Justices of other counties were allowed to do the same in the 1690s, but little was done with the permission.)

This was the first attempt at a turnpike, a way of maintaining the roads that will be described more fully later on. There was no shortage of people who saw the need for better roads and a few of them were prepared to do something towards improving road surfaces. The first booklet about repairing roads was written by Thomas Mace in 1675. The neglect of centuries could not be corrected overnight but at least something was being done.

Vehicles

Improvements to the roads encouraged a little more variety in the types of vehicle in use. Wealthy people could afford to have the lighter two-wheeled carriages with springs of tempered steel which became available about 1665. The body of the coach was hung from leather straps fastened to the end of C-shaped springs, the other end being bolted to the framework holding the wheels. These carriages were light and could bounce over rocky surfaces but were of little help in muddy lanes. They were more often used in towns. Gentlemen still preferred

16 A canvas-covered wagon of about 1690. There were no springs, so the passengers on their wooden seats felt every bump. The driver had a whip to keep the horses going but road a separate horse himself. There was very little risk of such a wagon going too fast.

17 A train of packhorses on a mountain track. The bells gave warning to other travellers. Each load was covered with canvas to keep the weather out. No wheeled vehicles could use such a track.

to travel on horseback, and they continued to do so for most of the eighteenth century; it was both faster and less uncomfortable. Some ladies also preferred riding side-saddle to being jolted in a carriage.

Poorer people had very little opportunity to travel, having neither the time nor the money; they usually walked if they did have to go anywhere. Villages and scattered farms were supplied with scissors, tapes and ribbons by pedlars and packmen who walked from one place to the next.

There were a few stage coaches on the roads before 1700, mostly run by Londoners, but they were expensive. The fare in the 1670s was one shilling for every five miles, and a coach covered forty to fifty miles a day. The journey from London to Oxford took twelve hours and journeys north of Oxford took longer because the roads were worse. Every coach took a set of wheelwright's tools in case of accident. The agent of the Duke of Newcastle once travelled from Hastings through Canterbury to London – and twenty men were needed to lift his coach over ruts and obstructions.

The movement of goods was subject to the same appalling road surfaces. Some goods did travel in carts or wagons, such as the hay cart referred to earlier. The goods carried were bulky but light. There were also a few stage wagons operating soon after the Restoration, heavy and clumsy carts which lurched slowly but cheaply along regular routes. They resembled the canvas-covered wagon featured in today's 'Westerns' and travelled ten to fifteen miles a day. Their iron-shod wheels cut deep ruts in the roads. More wagons were in use in the 1680s than ever before but they were little used in areas far from London.

The pack-animal was the main form of goods transport in all hilly districts (and many others) and remained important throughout the eighteenth century. The animals used were horses, donkeys and mules which were tied together in strings of up to nine animals. The leader had bells fastened to its saddle and the goods were normally carried in pannier baskets, one on either side, which held about a hundredweight each. Coal, stone, corn and everything else was moved in this way, though pieces of cloth were often draped over the back of the animal. In the mid-eighteenth century 500 packhorses at a time could be seen at the Cornish port of Hayle loading up with coal for the tin mines, steam pumping-engines and for people's homes. Men on horseback used to start their journey early in the morning to avoid following a slow-moving pack-train on a road too narrow to pass them.

Industries in the Pennines were supplied with all their raw materials by pack-animals, and special roads were made for them known as causeways or causeys. These causeys were about two feet wide – just wide enough for animals in single file – and raised above the mud of the rest of the road. Flagstones were used to make a lasting surface and any bridges along the route were narrow and had low parapets so that the panniers would hang over the edge. (Many stretches of these causeys are now public footpaths, as for example around Todmorden in Yorkshire.) Such roads allowed the pack-horse trains to keep moving steadily but led to difficulties when two trains approached each other from opposite directions. Part of the road from Glasgow to London included a causeway near Grantham: a writer in 1739 noticed one string of packhorses standing in a ditch for another string to pass.

The costs of this kind of transport were high. The price of coal in Manchester fell by half when the Duke of Bridgwater replaced pack-horses with his canal in 1761; his customers used to pay sevenpence a hundredweight. The butter used in Bristol came from Bath, twelve miles away; its price rose by four times when the road was blocked in the winter of 1738–39.

The state of roads 1700–1750

The roads were very bad in the first half of the eighteenth century. They varied greatly from one part of the country to another, the local soil having much to do with the nature of the road's surface. The best surfaces were the causeways but these were far too narrow for vehicles; where the roads were wider, the lack of a prepared surface made the going slow and painful. Many animals were needed to pull even a few tons – eight oxen and a horse were necessary to deliver a cart-

18 Part of a map of Bristol drawn in 1673. The city still had most of its old walls, and the gates in these made the streets narrow. High Street and Broad Street stand out from the other narrow alleys. The bridge (centre bottom) has houses on both sides and a church across it, forming a tunnel.

31

load of timber to a house near Leeds in 1700. As though the surface were not enough for travellers to contend with, the roads were full of bends and the lack of bridges added miles to a journey.

The bridges that did exist were very narrow. A survey of Yorkshire bridges made in 1752 showed that the main ones were twelve to sixteen feet wide. The widest was the Leeds bridge across the Calder, which was seventeen feet wide, but it was also the site for a cloth market until 1757 and traffic had to squeeze by as best it could. Bristol Bridge carried the main road from Somerset into the city. The bridge was almost impassable because it was lined by shops on both sides so the road was crowded with shoppers. A final hazard was a chapel built across the roadway, forming a low tunnel for wagons. The bridge was rebuilt in 1768.

In addition to the bad state of the roads there were the usual hazards of snow, flood and fog, and travelling at night was difficult and at times dangerous. One candle in a lantern hardly gave enough light to stop a pedestrian falling in a pothole, much less to help a rider or a coach. Many roads had no distinct edges and it was easy to lose your way. The vicar of Slaithwaite, near Huddersfield, in the 1690s, knew the local moors well but that did not always get him home safely. He wrote in his diary on one occasion: 'It was dark and a very thick mist upon Crosland Moor as we returned back. I was got out of my aim and knew not where I was.' At last he stumbled on a part he recognised and 'borrowed a boy and lanthorne to guide us over another moor.'

It may seem surprising that, with such an urgent need to improve the roads, so little was done. Part of the explanation lay in the fact that the growth of traffic on the roads was only gradual. Foreign trade and London's population had both grown steadily since 1600, as had the number of manufacturing areas and the amount of arable land. The union with Scotland in 1707 caused greater traffic on the roads leading there, especially on the Great North Road. Little maintenance work had been done on the roads during the twenty years after 1640. The whole system of parish maintenance of the roads was beginning to crumble and it had never been an ideal system at best. In the sixteenth century (see chapter 2) it had been possible for most men in a village to stop work at the same time and do their stint on the roads, because they were all tied to the rigid time-table of open field farming. Enclosures of farm land were beginning to be made early in the eighteenth century and, in consequence, farmers were no longer harvesting at the same time. It was inconvenient for them to have to stop all work for a week at the summons of the surveyor of highways. Also a growing number of men were employed in other industries and were unwilling, or unable, to stop for a full week. These changes were only beginning but they meant that the roads received less maintenance than ever just at the time when better roads were urgently required.

An increasing number of complaints were made about the roads from 1700 onwards. The road between Kensington and London, wrote Lord Hervey in

1736, 'is grown so infamously bad that we live here in the same solitude as we should do if cast on a rock in the middle of the ocean, and all the Londoners tell us that there is between them and us a great impassable gulf of mud.' Merchants and carriers now expected the parishes to provide a surface that was hard, smooth and well-drained, which were quite new ideas. Parliament continued to look on all vehicles as intruders on the roads, and tried to preserve the soft surfaces by banning all but the lightest of wagons.

Turnpike Trusts

At length the merchants, manufacturers and traders decided to act for themselves and bring the turnpike idea up to date. The tolls collected on the Great North Road had been put to good use and it was now thought that the idea could be extended. Accordingly the first turnpike trust was created by Parliament in 1706 and this kind of self-help soon spread; about 400 trusts were set up by 1750 and an average of thirty trusts a year were created between then and 1770. The process of setting up a trust and the powers it received were similar for all trusts so that a general description will serve. A trust began with a group of merchants, landowners and others interested in having a usable road meeting together to form themselves into a trust. The trustees applied to Parliament for permission to take over responsibility for repairing the road between two places. (Parliament would give permission to a group of trustees but could not do so to an individual person.)

19 Part of the Brighton-Henfield turnpike in Sussex, as it was painted in 1780. The chalk bank shows that the trust had made a cutting to lower the road. Gravel had been laid, but it was loose and rainwater had cut gullies in it. The grass verge allowed travellers to by-pass the road.

An Act was passed, allowing the trustees to set up toll bars or gates at each end of their stretch of road, and at intervals along it, and there to collect tolls from all travellers with the exception of pedestrians. The charges were laid down in the Act, varying with the size of the vehicle, the number of animals and the length of the road between one toll bar and the next. They were doubled on Sundays. The money collected was partly profit for the trustees and partly to pay for road repairs. The trustees were entitled to some profit because it was often necessary for them to spend large sums of their own money on urgent repairs and on building the toll bars and houses for the bar keepers. It was thought, however, that half the tolls collected in the 1750s were taken as profits, which did not leave enough to maintain the roads adequately. The trustees were allowed to take any stone that was needed, to erect weighing machines, to discourage damaging loads by high tolls or prohibition and to close any old roads that might take traffic away from their road. The Act laid down the period for which the trust could collect tolls (normally twenty-one years) and at the end of that time the road was to be made free of tolls.

The trustees set to work as soon as they had their Act. They repaired the existing road, sometimes employing an engineer like John Metcalf and sometimes planning the work themselves. They were allowed to use the statute labour (finally abolished in 1835) but more often they collected the money in lieu of labour and used it to employ old and unemployed people from the workhouse. Many of the trusts had no more skilled advice than the parishes, and some turnpikes were worse than the roads had been before.

From 1750 onwards, experiments were made to find a good surface that would drain well. It was then possible to find around London one road that rose to a sharp peak in the middle, like a house roof, another with waves of stone along it, a horizontal surface with a four-foot drop at each side, and a hollow surface which was washed by a stream being turned down it. Finally a convex surface of pebbles and gravel became standard and durable. The wealthier trusts also bridged streams and eased gradients.

Most of the turnpikes set up before 1770 controlled between fifteen and eighteen miles, though there were many exceptions. The average length of the fourteen turnpikes in the East Riding of Yorkshire was $17\frac{1}{4}$ miles, but they included a link road of $5\frac{1}{3}$ miles and the 52-mile York to Scarborough turnpike. Many of the early turnpikes ran into stiff local opposition, partly based on real grievances and partly on the dislike of change. The opposition might be a grumbling refusal to pay the tolls, or evasion by taking to the fields at the back of the toll house and returning to the road round the corner. Some horsemen jumped the bar. There were anti-turnpike riots, notably in 1726, 1732, 1749 and 1753. These riots were local rather than national but often very bitter. The events at Bristol noted in *The Gentlemen's Magazine* were typical of this kind of outburst:

Bristol, July, 1749. On Monday the 24th at night, great numbers of Somerset people having demolished the turnpike gates near Bedminster on the Ashton

And be it further Enacted, That all and every Toll Collector, being Leffee of the Tolls authorized to be collected upon the said Road, or appointed or continued either by the said Truftees or by any fuch Leffee or Leffees, to collect the Tolls payable at any Turnpike or Toll Gate to be continued or erected by virtue of the faid recited Acts or this Act, fhall and he or fhe is hereby required to place his or her Chriftian and Surname, painted on a Board in legible Characters in the front or on fome other confpicuous part of the Toll Houfe or Toll Gate, immediately on his or her coming on duty, each of the letters of fuch Name or Names to be at leaft One Inch in length, and a breadth in proportion, and painted either in White Letters on a Black Ground or Black Letters on a White Ground, and fhall continue the fame fo placed during the whole time he or fhe fhall be upon duty; and if any Collector of the faid Tolls fhall not place fuch Board as aforefaid, and keep the fame there during the time aforefaid, or fhall demand or take a greater or less Toll from any Perfon, than he or fhe fhall be authorized to do by virtue of the Powers of this Act or the faid recited Acts, or of the Orders and Refolutions of the Truftees made in purfuance thereof, or fhall demand and take a Toll from any Perfon or Perfons who fhall be exempt from the payment thereof and claim fuch Exemption, or fhall refufe to permit or fuffer, or fhall in anyways hinder any Perfon or Perfons from reading fuch Chriftian or Surname, or fhall refufe to tell his or her Chriftian or Surname to any Perfon or Perfons who fhall demand the fame, on having paid the faid Tolls or any of them, or fhall in anfwer to fuch demand, give a falfe Name or Names, or fhall refufe or neglect to give a Ticket to denote the payment of the Toll when demanded, (all which Tickets the Collectors of the Tolls are hereby required to deliver gratis on the receipt of fuch Toll; and fuch Tickets fhall name and fpecify the feveral Gates freed by the payment of fuch Toll,) or fhall unnecefsarily detain any Paffenger or Paffengers, or fhall make ufe of abufive language to any Traveller or Travellers, Paffenger or Paffengers; then and in every fuch cafe every fuch Toll Collector fhall forfeit and pay any fum not exceeding Forty Shillings, for every fuch Offence, as the Juftice or Juftices before whom the Information fhall be laid fhall adjudge; and fuch Penalty fhall be recovered and applied as other

7.   B   Penalties

---

20 Part of the Act of Parliament setting up the Buildwas Bridge to Watling Street Trust in 1820. The detailed list of duties suggests that some reforms were needed.

road, the commissioners offered a reward of £100 to the discovery of any persons concerned. On the 25th at night, a body of Gloucestershire people, some naked with only trousers, some with their faces blacked, destroyed a second time the turnpike gates and house at Don John's cross, about a mile from the city. They bored holes in the large posts and blew them up with gunpowder. Cross bars and posts were again erected, and chains put across the roads, and men placed to assist the collectors of toll. On the 26th between 10 and 11 at night a huge body of Somersetshire people came with drums beating and loud shouts, and some disguised in women's apparel, and demolished the turnpike erections newly fixed. On the 29th the turnpike gate was guarded with a body of seamen, well armed with muskets, pistols and cutlasses.

There were many reasons for the opposition to the turnpikes. In the first place local people resented having to pay to go on 'their' road – they had never had to before. (They became used to paying in time and some trusts had slightly cheaper tolls for local traffic.) Arguments arose about gatekeepers who were bribed to turn a blind eye to a coach going straight past the gate. Merchants objected that proprietors of stage coach lines had negotiated cheaper terms. There were continuous protests that trusts were dishonest or inefficient, both of which led to the roads being neglected.

The cause of greatest uproar, however, was the amount of toll charged. The rate per mile varied from one trust to the next but was denounced everywhere as too high. The following table lists the tolls that Parliament allowed the Hull and Beverley Turnpike Trust to charge when it was set up in 1744. The turnpike was $11\frac{1}{4}$ miles long.

Coach drawn by 6 horses	1s. 6d.
,, ,, ,, 3–4 ,,	1s. 0d.
,, ,, ,, 2 ,,	9d.
,, ,, ,, 1 ,,	6d.
Wagon drawn by 5 horses or more	1s. 6d.
,, ,, ,, 3–4 ,,	1s. 0d.
,, ,, ,, 2 ,,	9d.
,, ,, ,, 1 ,,	6d.
A horse	$1\frac{1}{2}$d.
Cattle, per score	10d.
Calves, sheep and pigs, per score	5d.

The additional amounts charged for coaches drawn by six horses show that the main worry of the trustees was what damage the heavier loads would do to the road surface. Tolls like that made sending goods over a long distance very expensive since they were imposed in addition to the costs of owning (or hiring) the wagon, feeding the horses and paying the driver. It cost £2 a ton to send goods the thirty-six miles from Liverpool to Manchester in the 1730s and £13 a ton was charged by stage wagons on the Leeds to London route. (By comparison, a craftsman's wages at this time were 1s. 8d. a day, butter was $5\frac{1}{2}$d. a pound and beef 3s. 6d. a stone).

The fares for passengers were no better. A Norfolk vicar called Parson Woodforde kept a diary in which he jotted down anything of interest. In 1774 he travelled from Oxford to Castle Cary in Somerset. The journey cost him £4.8.0, which included his meals on the journey, the tolls and tips he paid and the hire of post chaises. (A farm labourer's wage at that time was nine shillings a week.) A post chaise was a light fast coach driven by a postilion and such coaches could be hired easily on the main roads. Although it cost so much Parson Woodforde was able to do the 100-mile journey in one day.

Despite the high cost of travel, more and more people and goods were on the move by 1770. The population increased by about twenty-five per cent from 1700–1770 and overseas trade more than doubled in the same period. The volume of manufactured goods produced steadily increased, and the growing towns required supplies of food. Eight-ton wagons pulled by twelve horses were on the roads by 1750, and were the only alternatives to pack-trains and river barges. The owners of these wagons were encouraged to fit them with wide wheels to minimise damage to the roads. Many trusts charged lower tolls to wide-wheeled wagons, while the Broad Wheels Act of 1753 specified widths up to eighteen inches for the heaviest loads. Such wheels made the wagons slow and cumbersome and did little to help the roads.

Towns

More people travelled for pleasure by 1770. Private carriages became lighter and more elegant and fashionable ladies came to prefer these to the sedan-chair, although chairs were still popular. A sedan could be hired in London at a shilling a mile in 1712, and many of the aristocracy had their own. Each chair was carried by two men and was the best way to keep a silk dress crease-free on the way to a ball. The planning of towns in the eighteenth century, leading to cobbled streets and open squares, encouraged the popularity of the light, open carriage instead. The ladies wanted to be seen and to chatter – a sedan denied them both pleasures.

The other side of town traffic was the movement of goods. The streets of most towns where the above improvements had not been carried out were narrow, filthy and crowded with people and carts and wagons bringing food from the country. In Bristol, Defoe noticed in 1725 that, 'They draw all their heavy Goods on Sleds, or Sledges without Wheels, . . . and the Pavement is worn so smooth by them that in Wet weather 'tis dangerous walking.' Conditions were worst of all in London where 800 hackney carriages could be hired, adding to the congestion and traffic delays. In addition to all the vehicles there were as many lone riders

21 A scene outside the Theatre Royal, London, in 1776. The road is made of setts (square blocks of stone) and there is a raised pavement for pedestrians. Sedan chairs were still popular among the ladies.

as before. The authorities of Bath had to rebuild the main streets of their city because of the crowds of visitors arriving each year, and many other spa towns had to do the same.

It would be tempting to say that the better turnpiked roads had drawn the traffic and encouraged more people and larger vehicles to travel. While that explanation might be true of anywhere near a turnpike, the fact remains that the few turnpikes made by 1770 did not link up into a planned network of roads covering the whole country. Turnpiked roads were rare on anyone's journey before 1750. The Great West Road out of London, for example, had been turnpiked for the first forty-seven miles by 1752 but the remaining 220 miles to Plymouth were still in the hands of the parishes.

Quite apart from that, the policy of the early trusts was to mend existing roads, not to make new ones. Short lengths might be rerouted to ease the gradient but otherwise, the trustees contented themselves with widening and surfacing the old tracks they took over. As a result, the turnpiked roads were often no more suited to wheeled traffic than the old roads had been. It is, however, impossible to generalise about Britain's roads in 1770; some were excellent, most were passable, while some were 'fit only for a goat to travel', as Arthur Young complained in 1770. The time was fast coming when a more determined attack on the roads would be needed to handle the constantly expanding traffic created by the industrial revolution.

Case Study

A story is told in Marsden that the pews for the new church there were brought from Saddleworth in a wagon in 1758 as far as the hill above the town. There was no lack of volunteers to carry them the last two miles because Marsden people had still not seen a wagon.

It was in 1758 that the Act was passed setting up the Wakefield-Austerlands Turnpike Trust. (Austerlands was on the county boundary and the road from there to Manchester had been turnpiked in 1735. Similarly the road from Huddersfield to Leeds was taken over by another trust.) The preamble of the Act gave the reasons for improving the road, which was 'situated in a trading and populous Part of the County, and much used and frequented for the Carriage and Conveyance of Goods, Wares and Merchandize, Commodities and Provisions, made, manufactured and consumed in that County'. It should be made passable to encourage this trade but at present, because of 'the Narrowness and Steepness thereof in many Places and the nature of the Soil', it had 'become so deep and ruinous that in Winter and Wet-Seasons the same is almost impassable for Wheel Carriages'.

The new trust appointed John Metcalf as their engineer, nicknamed Blind Jack of Knaresborough. He was a remarkable man. Despite being blinded by

22 Communication between Manchester and Leeds was much improved by these turnpikes. The first turnpike, completed in 1759, closely followed the old ridgeway. The turnpike from Marsden avoided too many steep gradients, while the third turnpike (in use by 1821) followed the course of the river Colne.

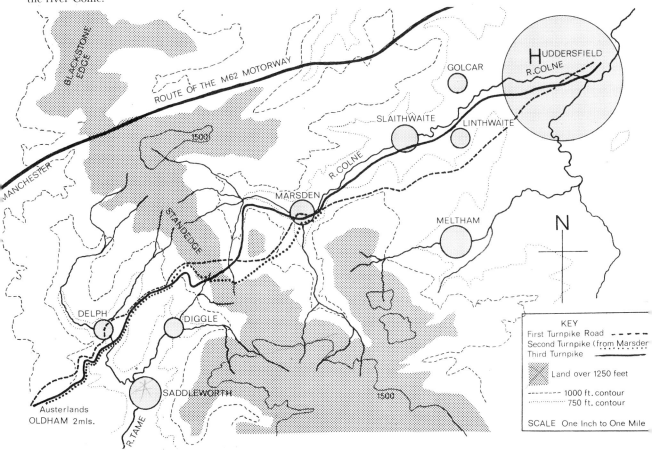

KEY
First Turnpike Road - - - -
Second Turnpike (from Marsden)
Third Turnpike ——————

Land over 1250 feet

------- 1000 ft. contour
.... 750 ft. contour

SCALE One Inch to One Mile

smallpox when he was six he had taken part in the fighting against the Scots rebellion of 1745, had run a successful business as a timber merchant and general carrier and had already been the engineer of another trust. He was to go on to build 180 miles of roads, mostly in the Pennines.

The route chosen for the turnpike was the old ridgeway. The traveller from Huddersfield climbed the hills on the south of the river Colne and only dropped down from them to go through Marsden market place. He was then faced with toiling up the side of Pule Hill, which was an ascent of 460 feet in a mile. The traveller had covered seven miles to this point, and the trust had only had to widen an old road and build two bridges so far. The route from Pule Hill, however, led across a marsh for half a mile and involved building a new road. The trustees proposed digging out the peat until solid rock was reached, which would have made a cutting that would have become blocked with snow in winter.

Metcalf thought this scheme both foolish and expensive, and thought out another plan. The trustees called a meeting to discuss the different plans but Metcalf simply said, 'Gentlemen, as you have a great deal of business today, it appears quite unnecessary to trespass on your time: I propose to make the road over the marshes after my own plan; if it does not answer I will be at the expense of making it over again after yours.' Nobody asked him what his plan was in the face of such an offer. A book written some years later described how the road across the marshes was built:

> . . . having sixty men employed there, he ordered them to pull and bind heather, or ling, in round bundles, and to lay it on the intended road in rows, and laying another across, pressing them well down; he then brought broad wheeled carriages (carts or wagons) to load stone and gravel for covering. When the first load was laid on and the horses had gone off in safety, the company huzzaed from surprise; they completed the whole of this length, which was about half a mile, and it was so particularly fine that any person might have gone over it in winter unshod, without being wet. This piece of road needed no repairs for twelve years afterwards.

The heather acted like a raft on the marshes, holding up the weight of the road. The fact that this stretch of road was so fine and dry shows how bad and wet most other roads were. The lack of repairs necessary was very different too; it was usual on most turnpikes to spread a new layer of gravel on the surface each year.

The road slowly climbed down from Stanedge, keeping to the hills above the river valleys as far as Austerlands, much as it had in the Colne Valley. The whole road was ready for use in 1759, which further underlines the fact that this was mainly repairing the old road rather than constructing a new one. Horsemen and pack-animals were able to move much more easily once the turnpike had done its work but coaches found it almost impossible to go up Pule Hill unless everyone helped to push. Clearly a more gentle gradient was going to be necessary.

4 The Coaching Age, 1770–1835

The Horsehay Iron Company of Wellington in Shropshire sent pig-iron to Chester, sixty miles away, in 1775. Instead of going direct by road, however, the iron was taken by wagon to the Severn and shipped to Gloucester. There it was transhipped to a coaster which took it round the coast of Wales and up the river Dee to Chester. The 400-mile journey was cheaper and quicker.

This company's actions, copied by many other firms in Britain, indicate how poor the roads still were in the late eighteenth century, despite the efforts of the turnpike trusts. It is also a reminder of the greatly increased volume and size of traffic that was then on the move. Many more people travelled, partly because of the rapid growth in the population and partly because of other factors, such as the enclosing of the open fields, which displaced people from their homes and caused them to move to towns in search of work. Work was readily available in the mills and iron-works which were the visible signs of the new industrial revolution. More people, and more raw materials and finished goods, made the existing forms of transport appear inadequate and outdated.

All forms of travel had to change to meet this challenge. Rivers were further improved, or supplanted by the building of canals, especially in the 1790s. Ports

23 The Industrial Revolution led to a rapid increase in the amount of traffic on the roads; it also provided the materials for improvements in the roads themselves. This iron bridge across the river Severn at Woodbridge was one of many that replaced fords and delaying detours.

and harbours were deepened and made safer. Heavy goods such as coal and quarry stone were increasingly moved on wagon-ways and tram roads.

The turnpike trusts, too, were caught up in the change. The early trusts had been content to put a surface on existing roads. Much more ambitious plans were now required to make the roads suitable for the heavy wagons and speedy stage coaches. A glance at the organisation of the trusts will make it easier to understand the variety of roads that they made.

Methods of turnpike trusts and parishes

The number of trusts was swollen by a further 600 between 1770 and 1790. In each case, every local person of any note was made a trustee. This meant that no one was left out who might object to the way things were done but it also meant that the trust was hopelessly inefficient. Meetings of the trustees were occasions for social gossip instead of opportunities for improving roads. Many neighbouring trusts spent more time and money wrangling with each other in the courts and Parliament than they did on the turnpike.

The trusts continued to have wide powers. The General Turnpike Act of 1773 allowed a trust to borrow as much money as it needed, did not insist that proper accounts be kept, and left them with full power to close old roads. A trust could almost do as it pleased; if a turnpike was not repaired it was still the parish that was responsible, not the trust. This grossly unfair arrangement meant that some parishes had to provide the statute labour to repair the roads, pay the tolls to use them and be fined when the roads again needed repair. Happily this did not happen to many parishes.

Most trusts maintained their road by what was called farming it out. Instead of thinking out what repairs were needed and employing somebody to carry them out, they made an arrangement with a local person to do it for them, paying him a lump sum for his pains. This 'farmer' seldom knew anything about road maintenance. He wanted the extra money, even though he had a full-time job already.

The arrangement satisfied both sides: the trustees paid over the money and had nothing more to think about, the farmer had a lump sum in return for work that he knew would not be inspected. The roads suffered, since the repairs were seldom done, and travellers complained endlessly at so disgraceful a way of spending the tolls. The consequences of these methods were listed in the complaint made by John Scott in 1778:

'The Trustees, when once a road is farmed, have nothing to do but meet once a year to eat venison and pay the farmer his annuity; the farmer has nothing to do but to do as little work and pocket as much money as he possibly can, he has other fish to fry, other matters to mind, than road-mending. Incroachment after incroachment takes place, the hedges and the trees grow till they meet overhead, the landholders are excused from their Statute Duty, and the water and the narrow wheeled waggons complete the business. At length, perhaps, the universal complaint of travellers, or menaces of indictment, rouse the Trustees for a moment, a meeting is called, the farmer sent for and reprimanded, and a few loads of gravel buried among the mud serve to keep the way barely passable . . .'

The financial affairs of the trusts display eighteenth-century dishonesty at its worst. The toll gates were farmed out, normally at an annual auction, but this was quite inefficient. The farmers did not declare how great their profits were, and they were themselves cheated by the men they employed to collect the tolls, who kept some back for themselves. The toll farmers paid more if there was a weighing engine with the toll house. These machines lifted the vehicle and its load from the ground, and overweight wagons were charged extra toll. The toll farmer made money out of the machines by allowing himself to be bribed, so that

24 This board hung on a toll house in Leeds where the turnpikes from York and Selby met. The toll house had a weighing machine. The top list shows the maximum weight for vehicles, which depended on the size of the wheels and the time of the year; the lower list gives the extra charges for overweight wagons.

TABLE of WEIGHTS
Allowed in Winter and Summer to Carriages directed to be weighed (including the Carriage and Loading) by the Act of the 4th. George the 4th.

	Summer 1st May to 31st October Both Inclusive		Winter 1st November to 30th April Both Inclusive	
	Tons	Cwts	Tons	Cwts
For every Waggon with nine inch Wheels	6	10	6	0
For every Cart with nine inch Wheels	3	10	3	0
For every Waggon with six inch Wheels	4	15	4	5
For every Cart with six inch Wheels	3	0	2	15
For every Waggon with Wheels of the breadth of four inches and a half	4	5	3	15
For every Cart with Wheels of the breadth of four inches and a half	2	12	2	7
For every Waggon with Wheels of less than four inches and a half	3	15	3	5
For every Cart with Wheels of less than four inches and a half	1	15	1	10

TABLE of TOLLS for OVERWEIGHT
directed to be taken by 3rd. George 4th. cap. 126. sec. 15.

	s	d
For the first and second Hundred weight (of 112lb to the Hundred) of Overweight which any Waggon Cart or other such Carriage together with the Loading thereof, shall weigh, the sum of	-	3
For every Hundred of such Overweight above 200 and not exceeding 500 the sum of	-	6
For every Hundred of such Overweight above 500 and not exceeding 10 Hundred the sum	2	6
For every Hundred of such Overweight exceeding 10 Hundred the sum of	5	0

instead of protecting the roads from heavy loads the weighing machines led to more damage being done.

These corrupt practices led to bitter opposition from road users, who also criticised the number of exemptions from tolls that the trusts allowed. All farm machinery travelled toll-free, even though it caused the worst damage. Other trades had privileges in some areas, such as the weavers in Berkshire who were excused tolls on their way to the fulling mill. Others exempt were local residents going to church or to vote in an election, the post riders, and troops and their baggage carts. Some trusts allowed unlimited travel in return for an annual payment; the Epping and Ongar Trust had people paying between 5s. 3d. and 21s. from 1769 until 1789, when they realised at last how much they were losing and stopped the concessions.

With all their faults, the trusts did improve the roads and set an example that many parishes copied. A Mr Lowe travelled through Nottinghamshire in 1794 and commented that, 'the roads of this country are of late years much improved, many parishes having learnt from the example of the turnpikes to form them properly, and have them executed under an understanding surveyor'.

Civil engineers

The surveyors were increasingly men skilled in civil engineering, as Metcalf had been. In the eighteenth century they were mainly self-taught, and they trained later generations of engineers. There were many such men, among whom two stand out as giants by their new ideas and capacity for work. Thomas Telford was one. Born in Dumfriesshire, and trained as a stone mason, in the course of a busy life he designed canals and harbours, supervised the building of 920 miles of road and 1,117 bridges in Scotland alone and was responsible for some of the major road improvements in England and Wales. Telford believed in building roads to take the heaviest available traffic, rather than banning heavy vehicles. He therefore laid foundations of heavy blocks, overlaid them with layers of smaller

25 One of the toll houses designed by Thomas Telford for the Welsh road. This one is on Anglesey. It is situated where a side road joins the turnpike. The board of tolls was placed in the centre blocked window.

26 The trusts could summon statute labour if they wished, but they usually preferred to employ men from the workhouse. Macadam had all stones broken down into pieces weighing six ounces; other engineers had their own ideas. The work was clearly back-breaking.

stones and surfaced the road with gravel. All the stones had to be broken by hand in the quarries or on the roadside. Men were employed from the workhouse for this job.

Telford was made the engineer of the London-Holyhead Road when the Holyhead Road Commissioners were appointed by Parliament in 1815. This 260-mile stretch of road took all the North Wales traffic and most Irish travellers. It was in the hands of twenty-four trusts, none of whom could afford to maintain it as a major road. All were placed under the control of the Commissioners, government money was provided and Telford allowed a free hand. In addition to resurfacing the entire road, he rerouted the Welsh section so that no hill was steeper than 1-in-20, and used the new idea of a suspension bridge at Conway and across the Menai Straits, the latter replacing a ferry. The scheme took ten years to complete and cost £750,000.

This was tackling the problem in a much bolder way than the trusts of the 1750s had done, but the increased traffic demanded such measures. Another of the leading engineers, John Macadam, was equally revolutionary. Also a Scot, and one who had travelled widely, Macadam carried out experiments to find the smooth, hard surface that vehicles needed. At length he found that if small stones were laid in three layers of four inches deep, all well rammed down, passing coaches and wagons ground off chips which made the surface watertight. The stones were rammed by hand at first, then by horse-drawn rollers. This surface made the massive foundations of a Telford road unnecessary, and it was cheaper to build and maintain.

Macadam was able to prove his ideas when he became surveyor of roads in Cornwall and, in 1816, to the consolidated Bristol trust. This trust controlled 148 miles, and found that the 'macadam' roads reduced the annual cost of repairs from £15,000 to £12,000. Macadam surveyed for thirty-four trusts by 1819 and, in addition to introducing his new surface to them, he taught them how to

45

27 John Macadam travelled 30,000 miles between 1798 and 1814, researching into the best way of making a smooth, hard surface. He was born in Scotland in 1756, and travelled in Europe, America and all parts of Britain. His methods remained standard practice for a century.

administer their funds with less waste. Parliament later made him a grant of £10,000 in recognition of his services to road maintenance. The methods of Telford and Macadam were copied and adapted by other engineers during this period, and many turnpikes and some parish roads were transformed as a result.

Major works, involving cuttings, embankments and bridges, were very expensive. Trusts repeatedly applied to Parliament for renewals of their acts, and these were granted. A number of trusts consolidated themselves to provide a larger income. The Bristol trust that employed Macadam had an income of £15,000 a year, while the Alston Trust in Cumberland collected £3,000 in tolls. Such trusts could afford the thorough schemes of the engineers. The remaining thousand or so trusts blundered on as they had always done.

Most parishes could not carry out improvements on this scale. They could not afford the services of a qualified engineer, and they adapted their schemes from what they saw done by the trusts. The work was still in the hands of the surveyor and remarks by contemporaries show that he was no better than his predecessors.

28 A list of Scottish tolls published in 1846. Heavy vehicles paid much higher tolls – work out the different rates for wagons drawn by two, three or four horses. Local farmers were charged less.

TABLE OF RATES,

LEVIABLE UNDER

THE GLASGOW AND CARLISLE ROAD ACTS.

	£	s.	d.
For every *Horse* or *Beast* drawing any Coach, Barouche, Chariot, Landau, Chaise, Calash, Chair, Taxed Cart, Hearse, or other such Carriage, each - - -	0	0	6
For every *Horse* drawing any Stage Coach, or Carriage of that description, - -	0	1	0
For every *Horse, Ox,* or *Beast*, drawing any Waggon, Wain, or Cart, or other such Carriage, drawn by not more than *Two Horses, Oxen,* or *Beasts of Draught*, each	0	0	6
If drawn by *Three Horses, Oxen,* or *Beasts of Draught*, each - - -	0	0	10
If drawn by *Four* or more *Horses, Oxen,* or *Beasts of Draught*, each - -	0	1	0
For every *Horse* or *Mule*, saddled or unsaddled, laden or unladen, and not drawing, each	0	0	2
For every *Ass*, loaded or unloaded, - - - - - -	0	0	2
For every *Score of Oxen* or *Neat Cattle*, - - - - - -	0	1	8

And so in proportion for any greater or less Number.

	£	s.	d.
For every *Score of Calves, Hogs, Sheep, Lambs,* or *Goats* - - -	0	0	10

And so in proportion for any greater or less Number.

	£	s.	d.
For every *Drove of Horses* or *Fillies* unshod, per Score, - - -	0	2	6

And so in proportion for any greater or less Number.

	£	s.	d.
For every *Horse, Ox,* or *Beast*, drawing Carts or other Carriages, loaded with Coal or other Fuel, Hay, Straw, Potatoes, Swine or Swine's Flesh, Lime Stone, Lime Shells, Dung, or other Manure, Grain or Implements of Husbandry; if not drawn by more than *Two Horses, Oxen,* or *Beasts of Draught*, each - - - -	0	0	3
If drawn by *Three Horses, Oxen,* or *Beasts of Draught*, for each - - -	0	0	5
If drawn by *Four Horses, Oxen,* or *Beast of Draught*, for each - - -	0	0	6
For Coals, if under Twenty-seven Cwt., - - - - - -	0	0	3
" if Twenty-seven Cwt. and upwards - - - - -	0	0	6

Provided always, that Toll shall never be demanded or taken from any Person for using or passing along the Road, or any part thereof, to no greater extent than Two Hundred Yards.

Extracted by

Clerk.

GLASGOW, *May,* 1846.

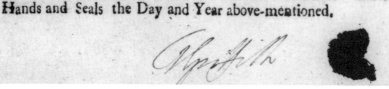

County of] At a SPECIAL SESSIONS held at *Mold*
Flint] in the Hundred of *Mold division of Hope* by Us, two of his Majefty's
Juftices of the Peace for the faid County, acting within the faid Hundred,
on the *17th* ——————Day of OCTOBER, 1797 *1800*.——

WE hereby nominate and appoint *the Reverend Hope Wynne*
of *the Township*
of Leeswood —— in the faid Hundred, Surveyor of the Highways
within the faid *Township* —— for the Year enfuing. And you
are faithfully and truly to execute the faid Office of Surveyor according
to the Directions of the Statutes paffed in the 13th, 14th, and 34th
Years of the Reign of his Majefty King GEORGE the Third, "For the
Amendment and Prefervation of the Highways, and for varying fome of
the Provifions in the faid Act of the thirteenth Year of his faid Majefty,
which relate to the Performance of Statute Duty," an Abftract of the
material Partsof the faid Statutes is hereunto annexed. Given under our
Hands and Seals the Day and Year above-mentioned.

29 Few parishes could afford the advice of trained civil engineers. Instead they continued to appoint one of themselves as surveyor. If the parish would not do it, the Justices of the Peace appointed someone, as here in Flintshire.

John Scott wrote in 1778, 'There are perhaps few offices wherein more skill and attention are required . . . yet before this officer is half master of his business, he is discharged and a fresh ignoramus chosen; consequently the work is never done as it ought to be.' Standards had not changed thirty years later when Parliament was told that, 'Parochial Surveyors . . . are interested that the least possible expense shall be incurred.'

In a few areas, individuals tried to make up the deficiencies. The Vale of Evesham Road Club was started in 1792 and made local travel possible again within a few years. Such enthusiastic improvement, however, was rare and short-lived.

By 1835, then, there was a network of turnpikes that linked London and the main towns, many of them having a reasonable surface. Elsewhere there were turnpikes of a poor standard and the mass of country lanes were still in the control of the parishes. Many of these showed no sign of the methods of Telford and Macadam.

Vehicles
The improvements in the main roads made it possible for the vehicles to be improved also. Wheels no longer had to flatten ridges into ruts, and the builders

of carriages did not need to make them so indestructible. As the carriages became lighter, fewer horses were needed to pull them, and yet the speed at which they travelled steadily increased. The golden age of coaching had arrived, as romanticised on so many Christmas cards. The stage coach drew the most attention, aided by the shiny, loud horn that announced its departure.

The stage coach was not new to Britain, but more were on the roads in the years up to 1835 than ever before. They provided the fastest transport available to those who could not keep their own horse and were widely used by merchants, traders and other professional travellers. They were still expensive, however, and so were the meals served in the hundreds of coaching inns along the main roads. An inside seat from London to Birmingham cost £1.1.0 in 1830. In addition the guard and coachman had to be tipped at the end of each stage, and this could add twenty per cent or more to the cost of the journey. The matter was big business, involving coach owners, turnpike trusts, innkeepers and blacksmiths. Three thousand coaches were in use in 1836, giving work to 30,000 men and 150,000 horses.

The speed of the coaches had reached its limit by 1820, when eleven miles per hour was kept up over long distances, with fresh horses about every eight miles.

30   The Sudbury, Hedingham and Braintree coach, painted about 1800. The body of this Essex coach was suspended on straps fixed to vertical leaf springs. Passengers on top had only low handrails to grip. The driver's box and the luggage boot were fixed directly to the frame – passengers in the boot were badly jolted.

31 Hogarth's engraving of the yard of a staging inn gives some impression of the noise and bustle that accompanied the departure of every coach.

This was a great advance on the travelling times of the mid-eighteenth century, as the following table shows:

London to:	1750	1830
Edinburgh	10 days	2 days
Dover	1 day	10 hours
Brighton	1 day	$5\frac{1}{2}$ hours
Bath	2 days	12 hours
Holyhead	3 days	27 hours

English coaches were the fastest in Europe because of the better roads. Three coaches continually raced against each other, the *Shrewsbury Wonder*, the *Hibernia* and the *Hirondelle* (more often called the *Iron Devil*). In the course of this racing, the *Shrewsbury Wonder* once covered an eight-mile stage in thirty minutes, which was never equalled.

Travel in the coaches was not comfortable. Those travelling inside had up-holstered seats, but the coach bumped and jolted continually. Those outside, however, had hard seats, all the jolting, little to hold on to, and the worst of the weather. The coaches had to start at dawn and go on into the night to maintain the speeds shown in the chart above.

Accidents and highwaymen were not uncommon, just to add to the dangers of travel. Mention of one accident was made by George Stephenson in a letter in 1835:

'I left London last night and arrived here this morning without the repetition of the upset I had in going up by the *Hope* which I daresay you would see by the papers . . . I never saw such a sight before, passengers like dead pigs in every direction and the road a sheet of blood. Two, I apprehend, will die.'

The brakes on the coaches were quite inadequate for the weight of the vehicle and the speed at which the driver tried to negotiate sharp bends. Overturning was the most common accident. Highwaymen and footpads were also a constant source of danger to travellers, particularly those in stage coaches. As the coaches ran to a timetable, it was simple for highwaymen to lie in wait, as seven did in Epping Forest for the Norwich coach in 1775.

Owners of private carriages also benefited from the improved roads, and slowly the choice of vehicle available to them increased, such as the elegant, high-wheeled phaeton which held two. Carriers' wagons also improved, particularly in using springs. These and the smooth roads greatly reduced breakages. Pack-animals continued to be important for moving goods, and many scattered villages still relied on the packman, as indicated in the following letter of 15 March 1788, written by David Thomas:

'I humbly beg leave to acquaint Your Honours that I lately travelled on foot from Llanroost to Conway in North Wales (nine Miles) with a bundle of mens shoes on my back, to wit, thirty pairs, when after my arrival at Conway I found myself excessively fatigued and unable to carry the bundle of shoes any longer being very old and infirm, and the weather and roads extremely bad . . .'

32 A mail coach standing outside a staging inn while the horses are changed. Since the mails ran to a strict timetable, the horses often waited in the road to reduce the delay to a minimum.

Mails

The improved roads led to far-reaching changes in the postal service. The stage coaches were able to outrun the post-horses by the 1780s – a letter sent by a post-horse from Bath to London took forty hours, but only seventeen if sent by coach. It was illegal, however, for coaches to carry mails. In 1782, John Palmer proposed that special mail coaches should be used in place of the horses. The coaches would carry a few passengers, travel toll-free and have an armed guard to protect the mails from the highwaymen lurking in lonely places. The first mail coach ran from Bristol to London in 1784, and within two years they ran on the main post-roads to all parts of Britain. They were advertised to run at eight miles an hour (including stops) and they kept to time. The driver of the *Quicksilver*, running from London to Plymouth, was fined £5 if he was behind time. This was a most important improvement in communications. The armed guard, together with the straight roads planned by enclosure commissioners, put the highwaymen off the roads.

33 The hobbyhorse was a mixture of iron and wood. The surface of the road, and the lack of rubber tyres, springs, lights and brakes, made for a hair-raising ride. Ladies were not meant to be seen on them.

Case study

The expansion of the woollen industry and the growth in the population demanded better roads through the Colne Valley between Huddersfield and Manchester. The main complaint at first was the steep hill out of Marsden. The turnpike trustees took the opportunity when renewing their Act in 1778 to secure powers for altering the road, and in 1780 John Metcalf was again the contractor for the alteration. The new road, a mile-and-a-half long, did not descend into Marsden and was therefore able to climb up to Stanedge by a much gentler route. This new road was extended a further mile-and-a-half in 1816 when the old road across the marshes was abandoned in preference to one 600 yards to the south. Similar alterations were made near Austerlands.

In 1820 work started on a new road that would replace all the older turnpikes. The old trust was dissolved and a new one formed. The first stage of the improvement was to build a road lower down in the valley following the course of the river. It was built on a ledge of the valley side, and ran nearly level for the seven miles from Huddersfield to Marsden. It was in use by 1821, and was much faster than the older hilly turnpike. (The second stage of this new road was not finished until 1839.)

The results of these improvements were swift. The first stage coach between Leeds and Manchester ran through the valley in 1789, by 1811 there were three a week, and six by 1825. The high point was reached in 1834 when nine coaches used this route. This opened up much better communications for local residents and long-distance travellers alike, and was a most important aid to the growth of industry and trade. Carriers' wagons also made constant use of the road now that it was fit for vehicles.

Despite such developments, it must not be thought that the older ways of travelling disappeared as quickly. Pack-horses continued to use the causey to Rochdale and the majority of people walked about their business. The weavers tramped to the Huddersfield Cloth Hall every Tuesday, carrying their 30-pound pieces of cloth on their backs. The school-master in Slaithwaite noted in his diary in 1796, 'Rev. Mr. Falcon walks today to Leeds and takes coach there for Cambridge.' The master, John Murgatroyd, himself walked the ten miles to Halifax in 1804, at the age of eighty-five, and then visited the many people he had gone to see. Going on foot was common in the area; stage and mail coaches were unusual sights. They were soon to become even rarer, and the efforts of the trust to appear wasted.

5 The Railway Age, 1835–1896

The turnpike trusts were most prosperous in the mid-1830s. Then came what Sir James Macadam called 'the calamity of railways'. The first signs of how serious a threat the railways were came with the opening of the Liverpool and Manchester Railway in 1830. The full effects of the railways were felt by the end of the decade, and the last mail coach ran in 1850. This chapter is concerned with the sudden collapse of the trusts and the slow change in road control that followed.

Collapse of the trusts

Stage coaches had the passenger trade to themselves between Liverpool and Manchester in 1830. The toll bar at Irlam on that road was let for £1,300 in 1830. Such was the impact of the railway that the same gate could not be let for £500 in 1831. Although the passenger coaches used by the railway company

34 A drawing that illustrates the complete conquest made by the railways in terms of speed, safety and volume of goods carried. The road surface here is still loose and easily rutted, and the horses are straining to pull the wagon up the hill. In the background the locomotive speeds triumphantly on.

were only adapted coal trucks, with no seats or protection from the weather for third-class passengers, travellers preferred the smoother and faster ride to the expensive jolting of the stage coach. There was only enough trade left on that road for one coach in 1832.

The downfall of the stage coach was even faster in other parts of Britain. The railway from Birmingham to London was opened in September 1838 and no coach ran by the end of the following year. Except in comfort, the railways left the coaches behind. The gradual improvement of the roads had reduced the travelling time between London and Manchester from four-and-a-half days in 1754 to eighteen hours in 1837, the fastest that horses could manage. The railway cut this to twelve hours in 1838. Merchants and businessmen naturally chose the faster transport, which was also markedly cheaper. The first-class fare from London to Birmingham was £1, and the speed of travel cut out the need for expensive meals at roadside inns. The cheapness of rail travel was made available to all by the Cheap Trains Act of 1844, which required a daily train, running at twelve miles per hour at a penny a mile, to stop at every station. The passengers were protected from the weather by then, a far cry from the outside of a coach.

The stage-coach companies were completely defeated wherever a railway line came near their route. As they went out of business they reduced the receipts of the turnpike trusts, which fell by one-third between 1837 and 1850. This was disastrous for many trusts, many of whom had been in financial difficulties for some time due to bad management. Many trusts went bankrupt and many more were reduced to stumbling from one crisis to the next. This often involved personal loss. The Wimborne and Puddletown Turnpike (Dorset) was built in 1841; in 1847 most of its traffic was taken by the Southampton and Dorchester Railway and one of the road's promoters lost £48,000. Railways were not built everywhere, so some trusts were still able to make a profit, like the Sherborne trust which could afford to improve its road in 1848. This was unusual, however. The great majority of trusts were brought down by the railways which took the long-distance traffic away from the roads.

Steam Vehicles
Some people tried to beat the steam trains with steam road-vehicles. The development of a horseless road carriage had started with the top-heavy three-wheeler built by Nicholas Cugnot in Paris in 1769. This was not successful, nor were the first attempts by the British inventors William Murdock and Richard Trevithick. Trevithick's first one, built in 1801, reached nine m.p.h. on its first outing, but burnt out that night. Although he built another, he met with no encouragement and dropped the idea. Other inventors added improvements over the years, so that quite a number of steam carriages were on the roads about 1830. In Manchester, for example, Richard Roberts built a steam carriage which took fifty people down Oxford Road at twenty m.p.h. in 1834, and Dr Church started a service between London and Birmingham in 1833, using what looked like an

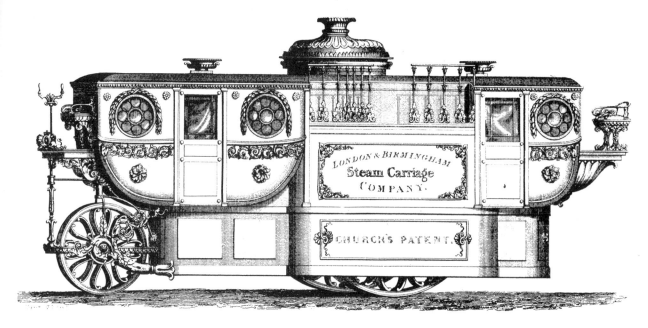

35 The ornate and grandiose horseless carriage designed by Dr Church in 1830. Its wheels were broad in order to flatten the surface of the road, and it was steered by the two handles at the front. The idea did not catch on.

ornate steam roller. Neither these nor many others could compete with the regular service in 1831 between Gloucester and Cheltenham using a steamer designed by Sir Goldsworthy Gurney or Walter Hancock's vehicles running between the Bank and Paddington in London.

Some of the steamers were reliable and went between fifteen and twenty m.p.h., double the speed of the mail coaches. They were forced off the roads by 1840, however, as a result of the hostility of a varied group of business interests who could not afford to let the new vehicles succeed. Tolls became savage and prohibitive, and represented the opposition of the trusts in alliance with the stagecoach companies and inns, abetted by the railway companies. The trusts might have found a new source of income in the steamers but they were too horrified at the ruts in their new roads to look that far ahead. The opposition to these mechanically-propelled vehicles took legal form with the passing of the Locomotives on Highways Act in 1861. This law, better known as the Red Flag Act, required every such vehicle to be preceded by a man carrying a red flag to warn other road users, and imposed speed limits of four m.p.h. on open roads and two m.p.h. in towns and villages. This Act killed any serious developments in passenger vehicles, except for the needs of the growing numbers of people in towns.

Towns

The rapid growth of towns inevitably brought greater traffic to town roads. The main roads of many towns had been laid with granite blocks or setts from quite early times, and this was extended. It was a slow process since the blocks had to

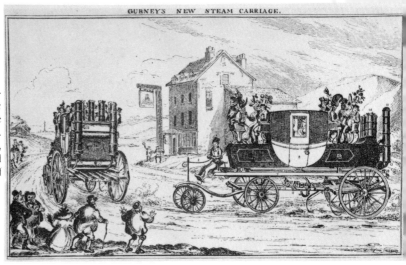

36 The steam carriage designed by Golds-worthy Gurney was less ornamental and more useful than that of Dr Church. It carried more people, and at similar speeds to the mail coaches. Opposition, mainly from the turnpike trustees, prevented improvement in the carriages; and the road itself quickly turned into clouds of dust.

be cut and laid by hand. Also such roads were very noisy, since wheels and hooves were shod with iron. Experiments were made with pine blocks, which were laid in Old Bailey, London, in 1838. These were much quieter, and the idea soon spread to central streets in other towns. Other experiments were made to find a quicker way of making up the surface of the minor roads. Tars from coal and gas were used to bind chippings from 1830, and bituminous asphalt was laid in Threadneedle Street, London, in 1869. These made good surfaces, but were difficult to lay until specialised machines were designed in the 1930s. Most town roads continued to be setts or steam-rollered macadam.

The movement of people within towns was another problem. Large towns had horse-drawn buses early in the nineteenth century (London had 3,000 by 1850), and London and Birkenhead adopted horse trams in 1860. These kept up a speed of about seven m.p.h., and were seen in many towns by 1875 (and can still be seen in Douglas, Isle of Man). Steam-engines were next tried, hauling a double-deck tram or several single ones which could hold 100 people at a time. These were tolerated in the industrial towns where a little more smoke was not noticed, but towns in the south of England soon abandoned them.

An alternative use of steam was tried in Edinburgh and other towns, where trams could be attached to underground cables hauled by stationary engines.

37 Many town roads were relaid with stone setts, occasionally with wood blocks, in the middle of the nineteenth century. They were banged down on a bed of sand or ashes with heavy mallets. In this drawing of the repaving of the Strand, the 'conductor' banged the gate to keep time.

38 Public transport in towns started from horse-drawn buses, because any development in steam vehicles had been opposed. The front two horses are being added to haul the bus up a steep hill in Bristol in 1895. Oil coach lights allowed the bus to be seen at night.

The final development was the electric tram, first used in Brighton, Blackpool and Ryde in 1884. This was clean and many municipal authorities soon began to use it in preference to all other kinds of haulage. Trams showed themselves capable of moving large numbers of people, and 1,000 miles of tramline were in use by 1900.

Parish roads again

The railways thus took over (and greatly expanded) the long-distance traffic, and any form of competition by road vehicles was made almost impossible. Main roads were no longer important, and the improvement schemes started by the trusts came to a sudden stop. Only local traffic was left on the roads, although the variety of vehicles in use widened steadily. The parishes had never ceased to be responsible for the roads and, of a total of 125,000 miles, the trusts had controlled no more than 22,000. The rest had remained the responsibility of the parishes, which began to receive back the turnpikes wherever the trusts went bankrupt.

This caused trouble. The roads belonging to bankrupt trusts had had little maintenance for years, so that the parishes were faced with having to pay to repair roads which they had already paid tolls to use. Riots occurred, quite the worst being in South Wales in 1842–3 where the men dressed in women's clothes and were known as Rebecca and her daughters. Matters were made worse in Wales by attempts to enforce statute labour and by the large number of toll gates. The Rebecca riots were well-organised, so that eighty gates were destroyed in Carmarthenshire, and none left standing in Pembrokeshire and Cardiganshire. Good came of it all, for the trusts were replaced by county road-boards. These could afford qualified engineers and made better use of the money they collected through the rates.

In England, on the other hand, no such changes were made. The General Highway Act of 1835 tried to improve the standard of parish maintenance. A

39 One horse could pull more people in a tram on rails than two could in a bus. Setts have been laid by rails but the rest of this road in Leicester is still macadamed. This was in 1902.

meeting of the ratepayers could now appoint the surveyor, and could pay him a salary if they wished. Statute labour was abolished and in its place the surveyor could collect a highway rate, as many parishes had been doing voluntarily for a century. The money was to be spent on hiring men to mend the roads, which was more likely to produce results than taking men from their work for one week in the year.

The Act thus confirmed 15,000 highway authorities (the parishes), half of which were very small. Parishes could combine into a highway district if they wanted to share a qualified surveyor, but most parishes were too suspicious of their neighbours to risk it. Attempts at this time to make a county the unit for road maintenance failed.

The Start of Government Control

The first break in the centuries-old responsibility of the parishes came with the Public Health Act of 1848, which made the local Boards of Health responsible for all roads in the newly created urban areas. This was a popular arrangement and the number of urban areas increased rapidly in the 1850s.

40 Some of the many uses to which roads are put are shown here. This road (in Bristol in the 1880s) is the way to reach the buildings on either side, a place to sell goods and also a main road into the town. The varied road-users mixed quite well at the slow speeds of that time, but motor cars have changed things.

It may seem strange that roads should be regarded as matters of public health. The fact that they were, underlines the complexity that must always surround roads. They have to serve such a variety of functions. As has been traced so far in this book, the road was at first a common pathway for the use of people living in a village who wished to visit each other and along which they carried goods. In time, the same road became the route by which strangers travelled, who might have no interest in the village and might not pause in their journey. Already there was a conflict of uses, for the villagers would want to stroll in the road, play in it, leave animals and vehicles temporarily, hold markets in it and treat it generally as an area for the common benefit of all. The stranger, on the other hand, wanted to go swiftly on his way, unhindered by pedestrians, children and abandoned carts.

The conflict was only apparent in the busy centres of the biggest towns before 1800. The congestion in central London was mentioned in Chapter 3, and the same could be seen in many towns on a smaller scale. The conflict only became a serious problem in the late nineteenth century, when the towns became larger, traffic began to move a little faster and the volume of through traffic began to increase again. All this change was brought about by the continuous rise in the population and the gathering momentum of the industrial revolution.

More uses for roads were found at the same time. The Public Health Act was concerned to provide clean tap water and remove sewage – where better to bury the pipes than under the road? Gas pipes began to be laid in the 1820s, and electricity cables followed in the 1880s. These provided necessary services to the

41 Drovers used to drive animals from the pastures to towns to feed the growing numbers of town dwellers. Each flock of sheep and herd of cattle was enough to block the road to other travellers.

people living along the road, yet the constant need to dig up the roads to maintain the services was a hindrance to through traffic. The problem has been intensified in the present century by the faster speed and greater volume of traffic, and the unpleasant fumes it produces. Indeed the problem has reached the point where a choice has to be made between leaving town roads for the benefit of the people living on either side of them or re-shaping them for rapid long-distance travel.

The Public Health Act led to improvements in many town roads. A Highways Act in 1862 tried to do the same for country roads by allowing justices to combine parishes into highway districts, each with a highways board in charge. The result was administrative chaos in a short while, with districts ranging from a couple of parishes maintaining forty miles to groups of 100 parishes or more with a total of

42 Roads are convenient places to bury pipes and cables. Here telephone pipes are being laid in Battersea Rise, London, in 1914. Other service pipes had been laid there before. Repairs to such services cause traffic delays, but where else can pipes go?

600 or 800 miles to supervise. Many parishes clung to their independence, even though they could not afford a qualified surveyor.

Ten years later another Public Health Act transferred responsibility for the roads to a new Local Government Board. Urban areas were left in charge of town roads, while elsewhere the groupings of parishes made to operate the Poor Law were to be the basis of road maintenance as well. This weakened the control of the parishes over the roads, and a series of acts and government orders continued the process until the age-old responsibility of the parishes to maintain roads came to an end in 1899. The Local Government Board that replaced them was no better, and is described in greater detail in Chapter 6.

Those turnpike trusts that struggled on to the second half of the nineteenth century did not last much longer. From about 1860 there was growing public determination to end the tyranny of tolls. All tolls were ended in Ireland in 1858 and the House of Commons Committee responsible for renewing turnpike acts increasingly refused to do so from 1864. Trusts were wound up at the rate of twenty to thirty a year in the 1860s and the roads handed to the local highway board. The number of trusts shrank from 854 in 1871 to seventy-one in 1883, and the last turnpike tolls were collected in Anglesey in 1895. This brought back the problem of parishes having to maintain stretches of main roads which they had not the funds to do, so the county councils created in 1888 were made responsible for all main roads and could contribute towards maintaining secondary roads if they wished.

Road users

While responsibility for maintaining the roads was slowly changing hands, many changes in the road users took place. The horse-drawn cart that was a novelty in the 1580s had almost sole possession of the roads by 1880. Animals mostly went to market by train, ox-teams were dying out, dog-drawn vehicles were banned and horse-riding was increasingly for pleasure only. Pedestrians were being given pavements in the towns, which left pack-horses as the only animals normally encountered. These, too, were fast disappearing, having advantages only in hilly districts.

The vehicles were very varied. The movement of goods over short distances was done in carts ranging from the low-slung milk float to the general-purpose brake. Some of the carriers were quick to link up with the railway companies, such as Pickfords who made agreements with the Liverpool and Manchester, London and Birmingham, and Grand Junction Railways. The fortunes of Pickfords grew with the railways. Other carriers carried on a local business, like the

43 A poster from the famous firm of Pickford's who were using two ways of transporting goods. The conditions at the bottom hint at some of the dangers of travelling by road.

CASTLE-INN, WOOD-STREET.

SET OUT

Thos. and Jas. Pickford, and Co's.

FLY WAGGONS,

Every Afternoon at One o'Clock, (Sunday excepted) to

MANCHESTER,

STOCKPORT, CONGLETON, and
MACCLESFIELD, LEEK.

And forward Goods immediately by their respective Carriers, to Bolton, Blackburn, Bury, Rochdale, Ashton-under-Lyne, Oldham, Haslingden, Leigh, and all Parts of the NORTH.

And every Tuesday, Thursday, and Saturday, forward Goods to

DERBY, ASHBORNE, and BUXTON,

From whence Goods are regularly sent to

BURTON-on-TRENT, WIRKSWORTH, MONEYASH,
KEGWORTH, MATLOCK, WINSTER,
CAVENDISH-BRIDGE, CROMFORD, BAKEWELL,
CASTLE-DONINGTON, NEWHAVEN, And all Parts adjacent.

CANALS.

GOODS taken in at the CASTLE-INN, WOOD-STREET,

And at Messrs. PICKFORD's WAREHOUSE at PADDINGTON,

From whence their FLY BOATS set out daily, and convey Goods to the following Places, viz.

MANCHESTER, ROCHDALE, BLACKBURN, BURY, BOLTON, OLDHAM, and all Parts adjacent;

COVENTRY, RUGELEY, NEWCASTLE, ALTRINGHAM,
ATHERSTONE, STONE, NANTWICH, PRESTON,
POLESWORTH, STOKE, MIDDLEWICH, PRESCOTT,
FEAZLEY, BURSLEM, NORTHWICH, AND
TAMWORTH, The POTTERY, RUNCORN, St. HELENS,

ORMSKIRK, CHORLEY, and all Parts of the NORTH; KENDAL, WIGAN, LANCASTER, WARRINGTON, and

LIVERPOOL,

From which last Place Goods are regularly forwarded to IRELAND, and the ISLE of MAN.

Likewise takes in Goods every Day for

DERBY, BURTON, and all Places adjacent.

☞ The Proprietors give public Notice, That they will not be accountable for any Money, Plate, Watches, Rings, Jewels, Writings, Glass, China, and Paintings, unless entered as such, and an Insurance paid, above the common Carriage, according to the Value, upon the Delivery to them.

All Packages of Looking or Plate Glass, Household Furniture, and Toys, are entirely at the Risque of the Owners, as to Damages, Breakage, &c. unless an Insurance of Twenty Pounds be paid on every One Hundred Pounds Value, and so in Proportion, at the Time of Delivery to the Proprietors, over and above the common Rate of Carriage.

No more than Five Pounds will be paid for any Package whatever, containing Lace, Silks, Ribbons, Pictures, Gauze, Cambricks, Lawns, &c. of less Weight than 28lbs. nor more than after the Rate of Fifty Pounds per Hundred Weight, for any Package of a greater Weight, unless it shall have been paid for as a greater Value, at the Rate of Sixpence for every Ten Pounds Value, at the Time of Delivery, in Addition to the common Carriage.

The Owners of Goods not paying or agreeing to pay the extra respective Price, will be considered as taking the Risque themselves.

Nor will any Animal be paid for, though lost, hurt, or killed, on the Journey, being the Perquisite of the Waggoners.

The Proprietors will not be accountable for any Accident that may happen to Carriages drawn at the End of the Waggons.

The Proprietors will not be responsible for any Articles that may be delivered to the Drivers of their Waggons at any of the Towns through which they pass, unless regularly delivered and entered at the proper Receiving-Houses appointed, at the Places above-mentioned.

Any Goods put into returned Wrappers, if lost or stole, the Proprietors will not be accountable for.

Any Goods addressed to Order, or until called for, if not taken away within the Space of forty-eight Hours from the Time of their Arrival, every Accident or Damage they may sustain, will be for the Remainder of their Continuance, at the Risque of the Owners.

Any Claim for Damages, that is not made within three Days after the Delivery of the Goods, will not be allowed.

The Proprietors desire that the Senders of Aquafortis, Spirits of Vitriol, or any other ardent Spirits, will write on the Direction the Contents, and make it known to the Book-Keeper at the Time of Delivery, in Order that it may be safely loaded, otherwise any Damage arising therefrom, shall look to the Senders for an Indemnification.

If Canals should be stopped by Frost, every Attention will be paid to have the Goods regularly forwarded by Land, and a Land Price charged thereon.

Vigevens, Printer, Huggin Lane, Wood Street.

63

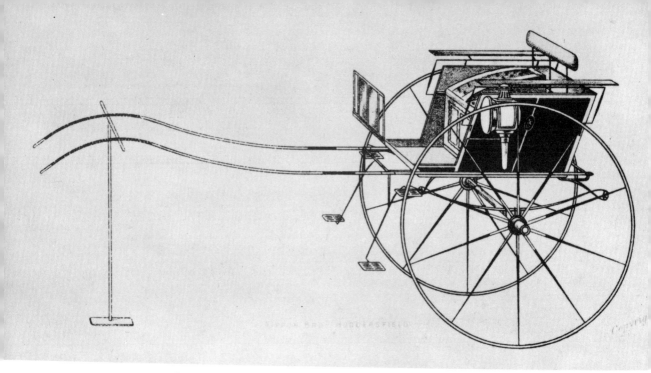

44 Examples from a range of two dozen light carriages made by one firm about 1900. The gig (*above*) was a lightweight, fast two-seater, pulled by one horse. The drag (*below*) was a heavier, four- or five-seater. Such carriages remained in common use among those who could afford them until the First World War led to more motor vehicles being available.

SHOOTING DRAG.

tranter (local name for carrier) who figures in *Under the Greenwood Tree* by Thomas Hardy:

'. . . as he neared the handpost at Mellstock Cross, sitting on the front board of the spring cart – his legs on the outside, and his whole frame jigging up and down like a candle-flame to the time of Smart's trotting – who should he see coming down the hill but his father in the light wagon, quivering up and down on a smaller scale of shakes, those merely caused by the stones in the road.'

Like the many kinds of coasting ship at this time, the carriers moved anything anywhere, at their own speed.

Passenger carriages also grew in variety and often in elegance. A look around the stables of stately homes open to the public will give a good idea of the range available, from simple two-seater gigs to the luxurious four-in-hand. The increase of wealth led to more families having their own carriage, often a clarence, and many had more than one. The ownership of a family carriage was common enough for Mrs. Beeton to include a section about its management in her *Household Management* in 1859. Part of it reads:

'. . . the coachman's office . . . is to drive, and much of the enjoyment of those in the carriage depends on his proficiency in his art. . . . He should have sufficient knowledge of the construction of the carriage to know when it is out of order – to know also the pace at which he can go over the road he has under him, without risking the springs, and without shaking those he is driving too much.'

A coachman was recommended to be paid £25 – £50 a year, plus board, lodging and livery.

These vehicles were modifications of vehicles that had been used for centuries: the traction engine heralded a new kind of vehicle that would put the others into

45 The first steam roller appeared in 1866 and this one the next year. The road surfaces were enormously improved by their use.

museums. The first traction engine was built in 1859 by Aveling and Porter in Rochester. It was soon followed by others, built by John Fowler of Leeds, Charles Burrell in Thetford and ninety other firms. Many traction engines were employed in agriculture but a number of general-purpose engines were increasingly used for heavy haulage. Above all the steam roller had a profound effect on road-making. They ranged in weight from six to fifteen tons and were able to pack a macadam road very hard. Thousands of miles of roads owe their present-day strength to the foundations pressed down by a steam roller. The rollers were fitted with strong spikes called scarifiers. These acted as a road plough and meant that, instead of patching holes, bad lengths of road were removed and remade.

The Red Flag Act was aimed at traction engines. Although it hampered their speed, the Act did limit the amount of tolls they had to pay. The red flag was no longer required from 1878 but the other conditions still applied.

Another new sight was the bicycle, seen in rapidly increasing numbers from the 1870s. The hobby horse had been known early in the eighteenth century and Macmillan invented the treadle bicycle with brakes in 1838; but the mass-production of bicycles only started in Coventry in 1869. Two hundred varieties were available by 1874. The penny-farthing was then very popular, to be replaced by the safety bicycle with equal-sized wheels from 1885. The pneumatic tyre invented by a Belfast vet, J. B. Dunlop, made cycling much more pleasant, and whole families took to the road at weekends, away from the dirt and dust of the towns.

The rubber tyres sucked up the dust that bound macadam roads together, making cycling unpleasant for cyclist and spectator. The Roads Improvement Association was formed in 1886 to press for better roads but cyclists were looked down on for presuming to use the roads at all, since they did not pay the rates.

More weight joined them with the advent of the car and motor cycle. These had been developed in Germany by Benz and Daimler, and some models were imported to Britain. Interest in cars was confined to a few enthusiasts since the Red Flag Act prevented any worthwhile use of them. The repeal of that Act in 1896, celebrated by a run from London to Brighton that is still repeated, opened the way to a dramatic change in the country's habits.

Case Study

The second stage of the third turnpike between Huddersfield and Austerlands was completed in 1839, nearly twenty years after the first stage. The delay may well have been due to borrowing the money needed for so ambitious a project. The old routes up Pule Hill were abandoned in favour of a long loop round the hill. The first turnpike was blocked by a 15-foot embankment and the second cut by a half-mile cutting sixty feet deep. The result was a road designed for mail coaches, where a climb of 670 feet was spread evenly along four miles.

The tolls that could be collected at that time had been granted in the most recent renewal of the trust's Act in 1831. The list may be given at some length because of the information about vehicles given in it. The charges applied between Huddersfield and Austerlands (sixteen miles).

For every Horse, Ass, Mule, or other Beast or Cattle drawing any Coach, Stage Coach, Landau, Berlin, Barouche, Sociable, Chariot, Calash, Hearse, Litter, Break, Chaise, Curricle, Gig, or other such like Carriage .. .. 6d.

For every Horse, Ass, Mule, or other Beast or Cattle drawing any Waggon, Wain, Cart, Van, Caravan, or other such like Carriage, having the Fellies of the Wheels of the Breadth of Six inches or upwards at the Bottom or Sole thereof .. .. 4d.

Fellies of the Wheels $4\frac{1}{2}$–6 inches broad .. .. 5d.

Fellies of the Wheels under $4\frac{1}{2}$ inches broad .. .. .. 6d.

For every Horse, Ass, Mule, or other Beast or Cattle, laden or unladen, and not drawing .. .. 1d.

For every Score of Oxen, Cows or Neat Cattle .. .. .. 10d.

For every Score of Calves, Swine, Sheep or Lambs .. .. 5d.

For every Carriage moved or propelled by Steam or Machinery, or by any other Power than Animal Power .. .. 10s. 6d.

46 A steam tram (right) waiting to start in Huddersfield. The engine had to have 'skirts' to the ground to prevent anyone falling in front of the wheels. Passengers travelled in the trailer, never with the engine.

Heavy tolls were also exacted if a wheel had nails projecting even by quarter of an inch, which indicates how important was the hard-packed surface of a macadam road. The width of the wheel continued to make a difference to toll charges. The threat of a steam carriage came from George and John Hanson in Huddersfield. In June 1830, their coach carried ten people at thirteen m.p.h. on a level road and at six m.p.h. up hill. This compared well with the horse-drawn coaches but nothing came of the vehicle, perhaps because of the tolls.

Coaches used the road daily on their way to Manchester. In 1835, ten coaches a week ran between Huddersfield and Manchester, with such names as the *Cornwallis*, the *True Briton* and the *Railway*. Five of them left from the Pack Horse Inn in Huddersfield, the others from the Swan and Ramsdens Arms. Carriers' wagons also covered a wide area, and went to Manchester to link up with south-bound wagons. Much of this came to an abrupt end when the railway line was opened through the valley in 1849, though some of the traffic had gone by other railway routes before that date. The turnpike trust struggled on until it was wound up in 1882, when tolls ceased to be collected.

In 1882, Huddersfield became the first town to have a tramway system laid down and operated by the town council. Horse buses had been little used in the town because of the many steep hills. A survey was made by the Hallidee Cable Company in 1882 with a view to having trams hauled by cables, as in San Francisco. Instead of this, steam trams were tested the same year and remained in use for twenty years. Proper services began in 1883, and were extended to many parts of the town. The engines were regarded by the council as 'a splendid success', but a traveller described them as 'snorting and rocking along the tracks, emitting sulphurous fumes and ashes from their chimneys'. They were certainly noisy and at least one exploded, but they remained in use longer than in most of Britain.

6 Transition, 1896–1940

The forty-four years covered by this chapter saw the victory of the petrol engine over steam on the roads. In the same period, road transport of all kinds took away nearly half of the railways' traffic, and a slow start was made on fitting the roads to cope with such a rise in the volume of vehicles. The changes took a long time, and the arrival of one new invention did not chase all older vehicles immediately from the road.

Petrol-engined vehicles

The repeal of the Red Flag Act in 1896 had been anticipated by designers in Britain. Men like Frederick Lanchester were already making plans, and his (and Britain's) first four-wheeler was ready in 1895. The new twelve m.p.h. speed limit led to a sudden upsurge in the demand for cars. Some of them came from British makers but, because of the slow start made by British firms, most had to be imported. Names like Daimler, Benz, Renault, Panhard, Spyker and de Dion Bouton were more often heard than Lanchester. (Charles Rolls and Henry Royce combined in 1906, however and produced the successful and costly Silver Ghost the following year.)

The cost of importing cars from Europe and the USA made them very expensive luxuries. They were virtually hand-made, with leather seats and much expensive brass work. They were also expensive to run, breakdowns being the rule rather than the exception. Petrol had to be fetched from the chemist – normally a task for the chauffeur, the successor to the coachman.

A small number of firms produced cars that were a little cheaper, by using mass production methods (i.e. having boxes of identical components ready and assembling the vehicle from them). One of these was the ten horse-power Wolseley designed by Herbert Austin in 1902, a reliable car that outsold all other British makes at that time. Other cheaper cars came from abroad, such as the American Oldsmobile.

The growing number of cars were joined by motor bikes, and by delivery vans, buses, charabancs and lorries. The steam wagons were also still in existence; indeed they did not reach the peak of their performance until after 1920.

These road users complained bitterly about the poor road surfaces and the many hills and sharp bends. Just as bitter were the protests made by other road users about the dangers and the clouds of dust raised by cars, by the councils about the destructive effect of rubber tyres on their roads, and by the whole body of people whose livelihood was threatened if motors took over from horses. The

47 A Milnes-Daimler bus used by the Great Western Railway in south Cornwall. The wheels were solid rubber. Canvas screens could be unrolled in wet weather but they made it dark inside.

opposing interests almost made it a war. Policemen crouched in the hedges with stop watches trapping drivers who exceeded the twenty m.p.h. limit imposed by the Motor Car Act of 1903, while drivers sought the aid of the scouts paid by such societies as the Automobile Association. The speed limit applied to all roads, not just those in towns, yet many cars could reach sixty m.p.h. with ease. Many years passed before the public accepted the new vehicles and before drivers came to respect the rights of other road users.

One step in this direction was taken with the manufacture of cheap cars in large quantities. This began with the American, Henry Ford, who started production of the Model T (affectionately called Tin Lizzie) in 1910. The same model was produced for seventeen years, in which time fifteen million cars were made. Some of these were used in Britain and were popular. Ford used the new production method of flow-production to cut costs, and was able to sell the four-seater car for £125. (Flow-production meant that instead of all the parts being carried to one spot where the car was assembled, the 'car' moved from one assembly point to the next, growing at each stage. This was later speeded up with conveyors.) No British manufacturer could compete with Ford. Two hundred firms made cars up to 1914 but not one of them could produce more than one car per man employed; in 1904 Ford was producing nearly six per man employed by flow-production techniques. Other manufacturers copied the example in the 1920s.

48 A London bus in 1913, driven by steam. The tyres are solid rubber and there was no protection on the top deck. The design of the bus hardly changed when petrol engines replaced steam.

Road Administration

Before considering those times, it would be well to look at the effects of the first generation of motor vehicles, up to 1914. Some effects have been noted already – the danger to road users, and especially to those living beside the main roads. The damage to roads was also serious, especially that caused by rubber tyres fitted with steel studs. These gave a better grip for the car fitted with them, but the studs tore at the hard surface of the road, allowing water to seep into the lower layers. Heavy rain and frost completed the damage. Many people would have liked to see all motor vehicles banned from the roads, just as similar attempts had been made in the seventeenth and eighteenth centuries.

The Roads Improvement Association thought instead that the roads should be adapted to new uses. The Association persuaded the government to order an enquiry in 1902–3, and its report clearly pointed the difficulties. Despite all the changes in control of the roads in the previous century, road administration was still split between 1,900 local authorities, and the number was growing. The authorities ranged from powerful county councils to poverty-stricken rural district councils. The Great North Road from London to Carlisle was under the control of seventy-two separate authorities, not one of which had powers to make a yard of new road to by-pass trouble spots. Most rural district councils could not afford to pay a qualified surveyor, and yet these councils were frequently entrusted with maintaining the main road in their area. At the national level, no minister or government department was responsible for the roads, so it was impossible to question the government about them.

The standard of roads therefore varied greatly from one area to another. Some counties, such as Norfolk and Hertfordshire, called the more important roads 'main' roads and maintained them directly themselves. Surrey and Glamorgan were examples of counties who looked at it differently – by having very few such 'main' roads they kept the rates down. Most counties came somewhere in between these practices. Devon, for example, employed the rural district councils to maintain 1,134 miles of main road, and left each to do it in its own way. Some counties, Lancashire and Buckinghamshire may be mentioned, went so far as to help the rural district councils repair secondary roads. The resulting variety of roads can be guessed.

The 1903 report would not go so far as putting main roads under the central government, but it did recommend that the latter should make grants to county councils for the upkeep of main roads. This would have reduced the number of authorities to about sixty and cut out some of the variations.

The body responsible for implementing the report was the Local Government Board, which had failed to do anything constructive for those roads transferred to it in 1872, and did not change its habits. It neither carried out the ideas in the Act nor spread information about the latest methods of caring for roads. Indeed, it did not even enquire what was being done by the different authorities.

The Roads Improvement Association grew tired of waiting and acted on its own. Experiments were made with tar to bind the road surface in 1902, and with tar-spreading machines in 1907. Berkshire and Middlesex were among counties that soon adopted the new methods, and by 1913 Britain had a greater mileage of dust-free roads than any other country.

It is easy to blame the authorities for their slowness then (and now) to fit the roads for the new users, but the blame is not entirely fair. Motor vehicles burst on the roads after half a century when roads had been secondary to the railways. There had not been any long-distance road traffic, and the years of neglect in road maintenance could not be made up overnight. The arrival of cars was sudden and no one could say for how long they would be used – no ratepayer would be pleased if money was spent for a passing oddity. Above all the cost of making motor roads was far beyond the old methods, and beyond most councils' pockets too. The cost of repairing urban roads rose four-fold from 1890 to 1902. Many had no foundations and had to be remade. The use of tar to make a smooth, watertight surface trebled costs again. Eighteen million pounds were spent on Britain's roads in 1913, fifteen million of it in England and Wales.

These are some of the reasons, then, for the slowness of the councils, who were set a bad example by the national government. Lloyd George said in 1909, 'It is quite clear that our present system of roads and of road making is inadequate for the demands which are increasingly made upon it by the new form of traction . . . the State has for a very long period done nothing at all for our roads.' This was largely a condemnation of the Local Government Board. To remedy this, Lloyd George introduced a graduated scale of motor-vehicle taxation in 1909, and a tax of threepence a gallon on petrol. A Road Board was set up the following year to spend the money on the roads. It looked promising, but the Board did not promote a single road scheme or build a mile of main road in the nine years of its life. Instead, it gave money to the councils to resurface roads with steam rollers and tar.

The Board might have done more had not the First World War put an end to such matters, and in 1919 it became part of the Ministry of Transport – one of the products of the war. The war brought other changes too. The manufacture of motor vehicles for the Forces greatly increased the capacity of the factories, which were ready for peace-time production after the war. Also many ex-army vehicles were sold after the war, enabling haulage firms and bus companies to set up with converted army lorries.

Towns

Some towns had adopted buses before the war, but mainly to supplement trams or the new trolley buses in awkward areas. London had 2,500 buses in 1912, which were driven recklessly and killed a pedestrian every other day. There was no national pattern about public transport in the towns, however. Municipal authorities which had just invested in one form of transport could not scrap it and have another just because it was newer, and there were 2,000 miles of tramline

49 Tramlines, as here in Bristol, were usually laid down the centre of the road to allow single track working with passing loops. But it only needed a few parked delivery vans to cause a complete hold up. Leeds was one of the few towns where trams were separated from other road-users.

50 Traction engines being used in 1938 to take a 90-ton transformer from Manchester to Ebbw Vale. The three engines represent about 200 horsepower. Such loads have always had to go by road – the stronger the roads and bridges, the bigger the loads. This road is still macadamed.

in 1914. As an example of the long process of change, the town of Stockport, Cheshire, electrified its trams in 1901, and continued to expand the system. The council bought its first motor bus in 1919, but this was for new routes. Motor buses did not start to replace trams until 1931, and the transfer was completed twenty years later. Other towns replaced trams with buses more quickly, others again preferred to keep electric traction but use the more flexible trolley bus; Leeds, Bradford and Aberdare led the way in 1911, and were followed by many towns, especially between 1925–39. In terms of fumes and noise, electric vehicles have certain social advantages in built-up areas.

The growth of motor traffic was so fast that laws to regulate it took a long time to catch up. The Road Traffic Act of 1930, imposed rigid controls on bus operators. Commissioners were appointed in each of the thirteen areas into which Britain was divided, and they alone could allow buses to be run on a new route, a new company to start operating or fares to be raised. This arrangement replaced 1,300 licensing authorities and stopped the pirate buses that had led to dangerous races between different companies, especially in London. The Act also required drivers to be insured against third-party risks, so that damages could be paid to passengers or pedestrians injured in an accident. The Road and Rail Traffic Act, 1933, brought similar order out of the anarchy between too many cut-throat competing haulage firms. These too were licensed, and the need for a new public carrying service had to be proved before a licence was given. This was a marked improvement, since before the Act carriage rates had been cut so low that drivers worked too long and lorries were not maintained in a safe condition.

Changes in the Pattern of Transport

The expansion of motor services in the 1920s and 1930s was at the expense of other forms of transport. Those years were mostly years of trade depression and the total volume of traffic was less than it had been in 1913 until a slow growth began after 1937. The railway companies were hardest hit. They lost half of their traffic to the roads between 1913 and 1934, the biggest single loss as a result of the General Strike in 1926. The pattern of the lost traffic was uneven. The railways still carried more freight in 1939 – 265 million tons as against 100 million tons by road and fifty million tons by canal – but much of it was coal and stone which paid lower rates. The cream of the freight had gone to the road hauliers, who could offer a door-to-door service, and could cope with smaller items quicker than the railways. The railways lost more of the passenger traffic, particularly those passengers only going a short distance.

Much of the lost traffic went to buses and coaches, the rest to the ever-growing number of cars. The railways could do little to save themselves. Their fares were made public, so that bus companies and haulage firms could charge less. The railways ran their own buses from 1903 and lorries soon after, but they were only to be used to complete a journey. The railways were only allowed to compete directly with road services in 1928, and by then the damage was done.

Delivery vans and lorries also ended the career of steam wagons, as motor engines became cheaper to operate. The number of motor lorries, vans and taxis registered rose rapidly. There were 53,000 in 1913, and the effect of the war in familiarising people with them and their suitability for the job can be seen in the post-war increase in numbers: in 1920 there were 101,000 motor vehicles; in 1930, 348,000; and by 1938, 495,000. The expansion of public transport on the roads also tempted many people away from walking and away from their bicycles. The number of passenger journeys made on Derby Corporation Transport vehicles rose from eighteen million in 1919 to forty million in 1939, and the increase was typical of other areas.

The reason for the change in habits was largely one of cost. Travel by bus was cheaper than travel by rail, over both long and short journeys. The railways' advantage of speed did not make much difference. Many people lived further away from their work, and could afford to travel by bus. The end of the tram came because of the congestion it caused in narrow streets and the difficulty of rerouting a service. Scrapping them may have been false economy because they were quiet and fume-free, and capable of carrying larger numbers than buses.

The cost of cars fell by the 1930s. Herbert Austin and William Morris set out to produce cheap cars, and succeeded. The more they sold the cheaper they were to make. The 'bull-nose' Morris sold at £465 when it was first made in 1920 (few

51   The Great West Road into London in 1936, one of the very few new roads built between 1918 and 1939. The traffic includes many small family cars, and is held up by some of the new traffic lights.

cars then were less than £600); by the end of 1922 a series of cuts had reduced the price to £225. This brought motoring within the reach of many more people. The Austin Seven followed in 1924, of which 100,000 were sold in Britain by 1938. The popular eight and ten horsepower cars followed in the 1930s, such as the Ford Popular, selling at £100, the Morris Eight at £142.10s., and the Hillman Minx at £159. Taxation favoured the low horse-power cars – a Morris Eight was taxed £6 a year while a Rolls-Royce had to pay £38 5s. The popularity of motoring was reflected in the rise of privately-owned cars: in 1919 there were 110,000 such cars; in 1929, 981,000; and by 1938 the figure was as high as 1,944,000. While many of these were produced by the big companies using flow line methods, there were still many firms making cars by the slower methods. Motor bicycles were also bought in large numbers, though the cheap cars led to a reduction in the number of bicycles after 1930.

All this extra traffic had to use roads that had altered little since the nineteenth century, apart from the tar surfaces. The Road Fund was raided for other expenses in 1926 and less and less of it was spent on the roads after that time. Some money was spent by the government – £26·5 million in 1920, rising to £65·5 million by 1930. This did not go far, however, and the only new schemes of note were the Tyne bridge at Newcastle, the Mersey tunnel and a start on the Great West Road out of London. The Ministry of Transport began the classification of roads into A, B and C in 1920, and made the county councils responsible for the building of all roads from 1929. One thousand six hundred miles of new A and B class roads were built between 1924 and 1937. But this did little to ease congestion or prevent the horrific accident rate.

Many attempts were made to advise and control traffic. The Automobile Association put up the names of villages on circular signs. The AA Handbook commented on this in 1933, when 20,000 of the signs had been erected: 'Until the advent of these village signs it was possible for motorists to travel scores of miles without knowing their exact whereabouts.' The Cyclists Union, Royal Automobile Club and Motor Union had started to put up warning signs before 1896, and some local authorities added to these from 1903. The Ministry of Transport recommended the use of a red triangle and a picture warning from 1930 – the rest of Europe had agreed on the system in 1909. White lines were used in London in 1924, electric traffic signals came in 1933, 'cat's eyes' in 1934 and Belisha beacons at pedestrian crossings in 1935.

All these eased a local difficulty for a little while but more drastic measures were becoming necessary. The division of use for a road had reached crisis point – was it for the benefit of local residents or long-distance driving? Would the latter have to be separated from the former just as railways kept to their own tracks? The Second World War postponed the need for decisions.

Case Study

The four townships in the Colne Valley, Marsden, Slaithwaite, Linthwaite and Golcar, had a combined population of 24,052 in 1901. Each was a separate authority (until 1937) and therefore each had to bring the roads up to motoring standards out of the meagre rates it could raise. This was an impossible task. The main road became the A62 under the Ministry of Transport's classification and was made a trunk road. The county council was responsible for its maintenance.

All other roads the townships had to maintain themselves. It was a case of working out the order of priorities and resurfacing a few roads at a time. Golcar Council bought a tar boiler about 1920, and roads slowly improved. Since pack-animals were still being used to deliver coal on the steep valley sides, it may be guessed that there was a long list of work left untouched from the nineteenth century.

The valley had its own car producers, like many other areas. Sugden and Sykes began to produce a car called LSD in 1920. As many manufacturers found, the idea was not a success. Profits in car production only came with mass-production or high-priced vehicles. Cars could not be both hand-made and cheap. Most cars seen in the area up to 1939 came from the main producers.

53 The widening of the Stanedge cutting in the 1930s. The truck took the spoil to make an embankment further down the hillside. Compare the large number of men with picks and shovels to the methods used on the M62 cutting (56).

7 The Motor Age, 1940–1970

The Second World War checked the growth of motor transport. Petrol was rationed from 1940, and attempts made to run vehicles on coal-gas were unsuccessful. The manufacture of cars was drastically cut, partly because of shortages of steel and rubber and partly because of the higher priority given to making vital war vehicles. Private car owners lost their petrol ration altogether in 1942 and haulage firms came under government control. Roads were mainly used for short-distance transport, the rest being diverted to railways. It was easier to repair bombed track than roads. Many vehicles were laid up for the duration of the war.

The end of the war brought a mass of problems. The roads were in a sad state of disrepair. The worst damage had been put right, but much routine maintenance had been abandoned, as had many improvement schemes. Vehicles too were overworked and lacked maintenance. The first five years of peace saw the slow replacement of bus and lorry fleets.

Car drivers who had hoped for freedom to travel after the war had to wait until 1950 for petrol rationing to be lifted. The following table gives some idea of what happened then:

Numbers of licensed road vehicles (millions)

	1938	1948	1958	1968
Total of all vehicles	3·1	3·7	8·0	14·4
Main groups:				
Cars	1·9	2·0	4·6	10·8
Motor cycles	0·5	0·6	1·5	1·3
Lorries & vans	0·5	0·8	1·3	1·6
Public transport	0·1	0·14	0·1	0·1

The dramatic rise in privately-owned cars speaks for itself, and was the main factor in the total increase. Motor cycles lost popularity in the 1930s. The renewed interest in them in the 'fifties was brought about by the arrival of scooters and small engines fitted to ordinary bicycles. These were very popular for some years until the small car reappeared under the name of the Mini. The steady increase in the number of lorries and delivery vans represented further losses to the railways. Specialised lorries were increasingly built, such as refrigerated meat vans, concrete delivery wagons and bulk tankers. These combined the bulk carrying of railways with the door-to-door service of the roads.

By contrast, the number of public service vehicles remained remarkably stable. The larger figure in 1948 was caused by an overlap between the last years of trams and trolley buses and the arrival of diesel buses. For most of this period the number of vehicles remained stable, though there was a change in the type of vehicle. The number of buses declined while fleets of coaches grew. The change was particularly rapid towards the end of this period and is underlined by the decline in the number of bus passengers carried – from 13,831 million in 1958 to 10,233 million in 1968.

These figures represented great changes in people's habits. In the first place, there had been a general increase of affluence in the country to allow more families to have a car. The spread of hire-purchase facilities undoubtedly helped. Also, more people lived further from their work. This was in part a cause and in part an effect of wider car-ownership. The use of a car allowed a person to live in the suburb of a town and to travel daily to work. In the London area, people moved to quite distant towns and made a round trip of up to 100 miles a day. This growth of commuter travelling led to problems of town planning that are considered later in this chapter.

Car-ownership conferred greater independence on families than ever before. Just as they were free to live far from work, so they could ignore public transport completely. The trend of villages dying as young people left for the towns began to be reversed as town-dwellers moved to live in villages. The greatest changes resulting from the independence were seen in holiday habits. Most people who went away for a holiday before the war stayed in the same hotel or boarding house for the whole holiday. The car encouraged people to tour instead. By the 1960s, many families had holidays on the move, staying at one place for a day or two before moving on to the next. This pattern was taken further by the steady increase in the popularity of caravans, particularly after 1965. Car and caravan together enabled many families to have more than the one fortnight's holiday away from home, and enabled many to travel in Europe who might not have done so otherwise.

Roads in the Motor Age

The other side of the growth of traffic is the effect it had on the roads. As has been said in the previous chapter, little was done in the twenty years between the World Wars. The continual growth in the number of vehicles soon made the roads crowded. The wear-and-tear on the surface was a problem in itself and led to experiments to find more durable surfaces. Special machines were designed for laying concrete, sometimes with reinforcing steel mesh. The normal materials, however, were bituminous tar and asphalt. Tar and chippings remained the cheapest way of maintaining the hundreds of miles of side streets and country lanes, and gave England's unclassified roads a high standard. Asphalt was widely used for main roads, where it made a smooth solid surface. It could be laid quickly

79

TRUNK ROADS AND MOTORWAYS IN BRITAIN.

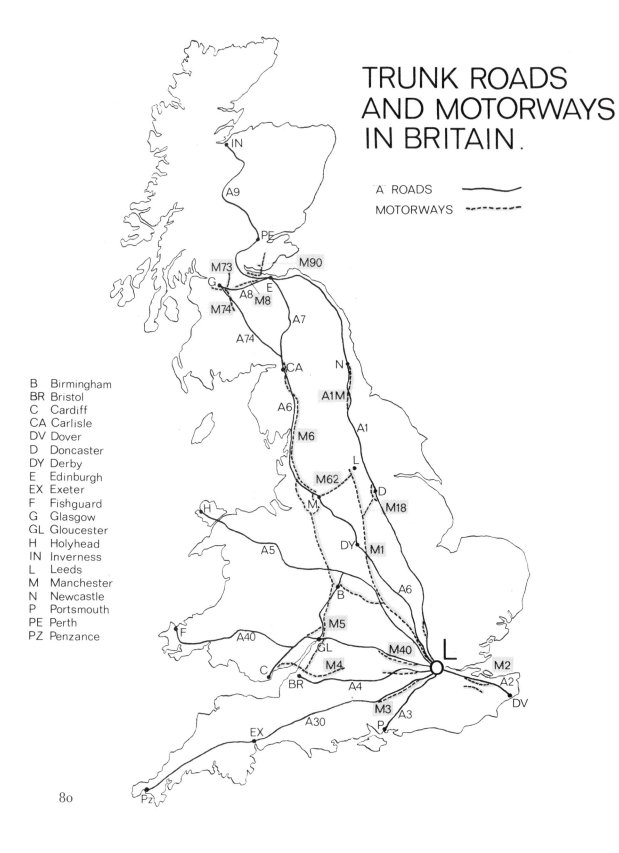

'A' ROADS
MOTORWAYS

B   Birmingham
BR Bristol
C   Cardiff
CA Carlisle
DV Dover
D   Doncaster
DY Derby
E   Edinburgh
EX Exeter
F   Fishguard
G   Glasgow
GL Gloucester
H   Holyhead
IN Inverness
L   Leeds
M   Manchester
N   Newcastle
P   Portsmouth
PE Perth
PZ Penzance

by continuous laying machines. Growing knowledge of soil mechanics made it possible to lay carpet roads, without the massive foundations used by the Romans, and later by Thomas Telford. Attempts at consolidating the soil with cement, so making a road, were also made. This would be quick and cheap, but has not met with any success for normal-duty roads.

The surface was only one part of the problem facing councils and the Ministry of Transport. The more serious part was the unsuitability of most roads for the job they now had to do. There were too many bends, hills, narrow bridges and congested town streets. A bend that was completely safe for a stage coach at eleven m.p.h. was dangerous for a loaded bus at thirty m.p.h. Men had once walked beside a mail coach on a hill, and even helped to push; their twentieth-century descendants did not relish pushing a double-decker and it was no longer safe to walk in the road anyway.

Somehow the road system had to be adapted to the needs of motor vehicles. Little was done at the start of this period. Nothing was done during the war and although £94 million was paid in motor taxation in 1947, the motorist saw little evidence of its being spent on the roads.

The first major bridges to be built in recent times were opened in 1955. These were the linked Neath and Briton Ferry viaducts in Glamorgan. This scheme was evidence of the increasing expenditure both on building new roads and maintaining old ones:

Expenditure on roads				£ millions
	1938–9	1948–9	1958	1967
Total spent	64·6	72·1	175·0	483·7
New roads	20·8	11·9	60·5	280·6

54 The two-level junction of the A508 with the M1 near Collingtree. Such junctions use up a great deal of land but make it possible for traffic to move at high speeds without worrying about vehicles turning across their path. Motorways take up more land than railways but allow a more flexible transport system.

55 The first motorway interchange in Britain of the M4 and M5 at Almondsbury in Gloucestershire. The interchange is in on four levels. Although it uses many acres, it is less extravagant on land than the American clover leaf interchange.

The new roads were principally the network of motorways. The rest of the money was spent on maintenance and on many small local improvements. The rate of traffic-flow on many roads was increased by the removal of bottlenecks. This might take the form of cutting through a double bend, or widening a bridge, or making it possible to pass slow traffic on hills. Road junctions were improved to reduce the risk of accidents. The Tamar bridge was built in 1961 at a cost of £1·8 million by the county councils of Devon and Cornwall. The bridge saved the hours of delay caused by an overworked ferry.

All such improvements helped but were quite unable to cope with the sharp increase in the number of vehicles moving between the main towns. Industry was increasingly relying on road transport to supply raw materials or take goods to the docks, and firms could not afford to have lorries stuck in traffic jams for hour after hour.

A programme of motorway building began in 1956 to cut through this problem, and the first stretch of the M1 (London–Birmingham) was opened in 1959. Motorways were the first roads designed exclusively for motor vehicles that could maintain a reasonable speed in safety. There were to be no animals or pedestrians, no parked cars at the roadside and the minimum of access points. All traffic was to join and leave a motorway on the left, there was to be no cutting across other traffic. The roads avoided the dual use of general-purpose roads by separating the through vehicles from the local residents.

The construction of the motorways was planned in a far grander way than roads had been for centuries. The bold building of roads through very difficult terrain was close to the work of the Roman engineers. The roads were different in all other respects, however. They were not straight. Gentle bends were deliberately planned even in the rare places where it would be possible for the road to go straight. The reason for the curves was to give the driver something to concentrate on, to prevent his mind from wandering. The motorways could not have the steep hills that the Roman pack-horse could take in its stride, because it was intended that traffic on these roads would keep a steady speed throughout. Deep cuttings were therefore made through hills and the waste used to build embankments across valleys.

Many bridges had to be built to take other roads across the motorways, and to fit in with rivers, canals and railway lines. The whole road was elevated on concrete pillars when passing through built-up areas, as the M4 in London and the M5/M6 link through Birmingham. Pre-stressed concrete beams speeded up the construction of these viaducts. Many of the bridges had to be built in very difficult situations and under strict conditions. The Barton high level bridge over the Manchester Ship Canal on the M62 west of Manchester had to fit the following daunting requirements:

'There was the need to design a bridge that would carry both 180-ton abnormal and 260-ton super-abnormal Ministry of Transport loads at a height rising to 100 feet above land where rock could not be found and groundwater would be troublesome and where some degree of settlement must be allowed for; a bridge of great length on a horizontal curve subject to severe load drag and wind pressures but capable of speedy erection and easy maintenance without causing interruption to shipping or railway traffic which could not be stopped.'

56 Excavating the deepest of the cuttings on the M62. The pile-drivers on the sky line bored shot holes for explosives, while excavators on two levels cleared the resulting debris. The finished slope of the bank can be seen taking shape in the foreground.

57 The Severn bridge links England and Wales at a point where other crossings have been made, such as the electricity cables. The ruins of the slipway for the old car ferry can be seen in the foreground. Each of the towers is 450 feet high and the span between them is 3,240 feet.

Some special motorway bridges presented old problems on a massive scale, in particular the long Forth and Severn bridges. The Forth bridge in Scotland was opened in 1964 and had a central span of 3,300 feet. The Severn bridge was finished two years later, and the span was sixty feet less. Both are suspension bridges of a new and graceful kind.

Motorways could not be built everywhere at once. The cost was £1 million a mile on average while the giant bridges were in a class of their own. (The Forth bridge cost £19·5 million.) A programme of improvements to main roads also accelerated during these years. The longest example was the gradual upgrading of the A1, the Great North Road of centuries past. By-passes of motorway standard, as around Alnwick in Northumberland, were built to relieve narrow streets of the heavy traffic between Scotland and England. Some stretches were made completely into motorway and many road junctions were avoided by flyover bridges. Similar work was done to many sections of other roads, so that slowly the national road system began to cope with the amount of traffic. The flow of traffic was helped by the setting up of standardized signs giving clear and advance warning of turnings.

The motorways and other main roads became excellent for traffic moving between towns. However, as these roads developed, the congestion in the big cities became fearful. Widening city roads is very costly and also involves uprooting people from their homes to clear sufficient space. Town councils were at first left to cope with the problem by themselves, so that many improvements in the 1950s were little more than easing corners and using complex one-way systems to give the effect of wider roads. Some government money was made available in the 'sixties and expressways, ring roads and urban motorways began to be built.

These new roads improved the flow of traffic considerably. They also made town life for residents very different, as had the whole growth of traffic. In many towns roads became divisive, so that people living on one side had little contact with those living on the other. This only took place on the main roads through a town but that could involve many hundreds of families. Through traffic was winning in the tug-of-war over who the roads were for, while local communities were losing.

In most towns the main roads meet in the centre, which is also where most of the interesting buildings have been. Many towns saw fit to remove some of them to make room for roundabouts and multi-lane highways. This was at a time when towns came to measure their importance by the number of chain stores that had built branches there. It was not long before the centres of most towns became modern, and also dull, lifeless and standardized. There was little space for people to live, so that the heart of the town beat furiously from nine to five, and nearly stopped at night.

Some people had foreseen this problem. An enquiry was made in the 1950s into town life and traffic by a committee headed by Professor Buchanan. The report, published in 1958, was called *Mixed blessing: the motor in Britain*, and part of it read:

'The danger is that we may set our sights too low, that seeing the problem as no more than keeping traffic on the move we may take a middle course of piece-meal street widening with ever larger roundabouts, gradually tearing the hearts out of our towns. It is not traffic movement but civilised town life that is at stake.'

Some towns agreed and tried to find a compromise that would suit their particular circumstances. In York, for example, plans were made to encourage families to return to living in the city. The old walls and narrow gates helped since they encouraged through traffic to go around the outside. Still in Yorkshire, the Leeds council drew up plans to halt much of the traffic at large parks at a distance

58 The size of the cranes and the mass of scaffolding indicate the scale of the present motorway programme. The scaffolding rises 150 feet from the ground and the Brown Cow bridge in Yorkshire is the longest concrete arch span in the country.

from the centre. Express buses would take people the rest of the way. Coventry's wartime damage was turned to advantage. The new shopping centre was built for pedestrians only, all traffic being taken around the outside. A multi-storey car-park was part of the scheme since the parking of cars in any town restricts the width of the road unless somewhere off the street can be found. Many towns followed the Coventry idea, though there were some (Bristol for example) who rebuilt on the same road pattern as existed in the seventeenth century, accentuating the conflict between traveller and shopper.

Throughout this period there was one sombre cloud – the rate of accidents. The following table shows the figures approximately corresponding to the volume of traffic:

	1938	1948	1958	1968
Dead	6,648	4,513	5,970	6,810
Injured	226,711	148,884	293,797	342,398

The rate of increase was not as great as the increase of traffic. Efforts to reduce the tragic loss of life met with little permanent success, despite shock advertising at one extreme and the 'breathalyser' at the other. Many of the crashes were not strictly 'accidents', that is they could have been prevented if care had been taken.

Case study

Traffic on the A62 increased in this period, in common with main roads in the rest of Britain. The bulk of the traffic was long-distance lorries using this part of the main road from Liverpool to Hull. 4,000 lorries a day used the road in 1970, making it difficult and dangerous for people to cross. Marsden was cut in two in this way and a ring road was started in Huddersfield to keep the heavy traffic away from the shopping area.

It was decided that a motorway was necessary across the Pennines and that this would reduce the heavy traffic on this part of the A62 by sixty per cent. The route chosen went to the north of Oldham and then through the hills to the west of Huddersfield. Marsh and moorland, hills and valleys were taken as they came, requiring many deep cuttings and high embankments. The opportunity was taken to use the waste from two cuttings to build the biggest earth dam in Britain, which both stores water for the area and carries the motorway across the valley. Many bridges have had to be made across the M62, including a graceful one at the aptly-named Windy Ridge to carry the Pennine Way over the road.

This, the latest road in the area, has more in common with the early roads than with the A62. The Bronze Age track and Roman road both ignored the valley and the settlements, as the motorway does, and local residents must again go to the nearest access point to use the road. They will prefer that and the quieter roads in their towns to having the road go past their front doors.

8 The Way Ahead

You may have gained the impression, having read this book from the beginning, that the roads and their traffic affect each other. The need for more wagons to travel faster in the eighteenth century led to the improved roads laid by the turnpike trusts. These smooth surfaces allowed coach designers to make their vehicles lighter and thereby get the maximum speed from a horse. The roads also encouraged the steam-vehicle inventors, who might well have met with more success had they not been priced off the roads. It is possible to trace such a pattern in road development from early times to the present, where an improvement in roads had led to a corresponding improvement in traffic. It has been more like a game of leapfrog, since the improvements have often gone beyond what was necessary, so stimulating fresh invention.

The times of improvement, the 'leaps', have often coincided with major alterations in the country's economy. More and better transport has been demanded and the designers have tried to cope. Invention, however, cannot be switched on like a light. Frequently the roads have been patched as best they could, only to be battered to pieces again by traffic. Then an inventor has appeared with the imagination to find a new method. The problem has seldom been solved even at that moment, however, for the new method still has to be implemented. This requires the confidence of the authorities and much money. It also takes time, since there are today about 150,000 miles of road in Britain.

In the years ahead some changes can be predicted with reasonable certainty. Some parts of the motorways are already choked by traffic, which comes to a standstill on the southern section of the M1 on occasions. The use of the larger container lorries and the increasing custom of moving large sections of machinery by road will clearly aggravate this clogging. Equally the number of private vehicles continues to rise. A motorway will only be able to hold a given volume of traffic, depending on the number of carriageways it has.

One way round motorway congestion would be to increase the number of carriageways. Four- and six-lane highways are not unusual in America, where land is of course more plentiful than in this country. The financial cost of buying sufficient land in Britain to widen existing motorways would be very great, but the loss of the land for other uses might be an even greater deterrent. Another solution might be to make the motorways two-tier. Something like this already happens in London. The M4 is built on concrete stilts, while another road for local traffic continues underneath. This idea could be extended to motorways, with the present road used for long distance traffic. The top level could be used by traffic travelling a very long distance. Fewer access points would be provided, so that

59 The elevated section of the M4 at Brentford, London. In the upper part of the picture, the motorway has been built above the existing main road. This method could be used in building future motorways, especially those that enter the large cities.

drivers might well return to ground level and use the lower motorway for a time before returning to 'normal' roads. Now that crash barriers are at long last being installed, it might be possible to allow speeds above seventy m.p.h. in safety.

Suggestions have been made that vehicles might become partially automated on motorways. This would be based on the device used in some washing machines of a programme that is slotted in. It would give instructions as to how far to go before turning off, and the required speed. The car's computer would deal with those instructions using information obtained from signal posts at intervals, and would also work out the safe distance needed from other traffic. The driver would be able to take control any time it became necessary. The use of such an auto-pilot would allow greater speed and, perhaps, persuade a driver to rest when fatigued.

It is useless to send more traffic faster along the motorways until ways of absorbing it all can be developed in the towns. This requires more attention at the present time than movement between towns. It is a difficult problem. The railways can develop their 150 m.p.h. trains because the journey ends in a station – the passenger must there get out and continue his journey by a different kind of transport. The road vehicle, however, travels at speed on the motorway, leaves at a junction and becomes part of local traffic on urban roads. Leaving aside the problem of whether a driver can adapt himself to the change quickly, there is a difficulty in planning towns to meet this change. The new town of Cumbernauld near Glasgow has incorporated motorways to keep traffic moving as long as possible before it turns on to the roads that serve the shops and homes.

There lies the problem. A driver with a van of biscuits will proceed very rapidly from the factory to the town where he has to deliver them. Being a stranger in the town, he will follow the roads to the centre and gradually go slower as he looks for the street he needs. Once in the street, he will crawl along looking for the shop where he must deliver his goods. Town traffic is bound to move at a slower pace as people go about their business.

It is the old problem, that roads have a dual purpose. In a town, people have as much right to walk across a road as vehicles have to move along it. The movements of each may be regulated with lights, but each has their rights and their duties not to be a danger to others. The solution to so thorny a problem would seem to lie in separating the competing road-users. The use of many layers to a road would seem possible in this also. A system could be imagined where pedest-

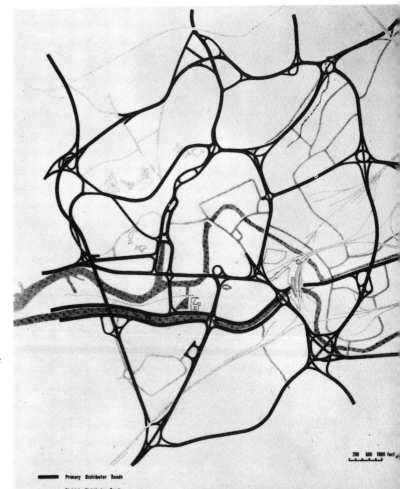

60 The shape of Bristol's roads under a 15-year scheme due to be completed in 1981. It will at least allow rapid movement around the city, if not into it. Public transport will be extended to take people into the centre.

200   600   1000 feet

Primary Distributor Roads
District Distributor Roads

61 The difficulty remains. This view of central London shows a maze of roads, along which people live. Where and how is the compromise to be made between rapid movement for traffic and a place for people to live?

rians moved on one layer where the shops were, while vehicles moved on another. The vehicles could further be separated, so that those wishing to speed out of town could travel on a different level from the local traffic of delivery vans, buses and cars. Pedestrians might be provided with moving pavements and escalators.

There are many difficulties in the way of so complex a scheme. A mass of road layers could obscure buildings and make visiting a town a nightmare. Towns might be drowned in roads. The amount of demolition might be costly and also slice hrough communities. Banning all traffic from historic town centres might help, but care would have to be taken not to impose hardships on some people. Young and energetic people would not mind walking from the centre to a perimeter car park, but it would be different for a disabled person. Nor would the provision of public transport help everyone. A mother for instance, surrounded by young children, would be handicapped by having to carry the week's shopping on and off buses. But as new towns are built so a multi-layer road system could be incorporated into them better than into old towns.

The movement of goods might be helped in a different way. The Post Office designed machinery to sort parcels in 1960 which uses a number of platforms moving on rails. The sorter is able to dial a code into the base of the platform which allows a parcel to fall down a chute into the right sack. The idea could be adapted for delivering goods in towns. For example, delivery vans could be required to go to a few receiving bays in a town, and from there the goods could be forwarded to shops by moving platforms. Shops could use similar machines to deliver goods to perimeter car parks, or even further afield.

Many ways could be found to reduce the amount of traffic in towns and yet improve transport for the convenience of people. Hovercraft run by computers and travelling over a concrete track of their own have been suggested as a rapid link between London and its airport. The idea could well be taken over longer distances. Electric trams might still have a future because of their speed and load-carrying capabilities. They might become cheaper to run if nuclear power makes electricity cheaper.

This introduces the matter of clean air. The exhaust fumes from vehicles in town centres are a menace to health. Electric traction is both cleaner and quieter. The electric car should become common in towns as soon as a suitable battery can be found. In the meanwhile, steam-powered cars would seem to have considerable advantages over petrol and diesel engines.

So far, this chapter has concerned itself solely with Britain's roads, but the rest of Europe can no longer be ignored. Plans to build a tunnel under the English Channel to France were drawn up in 1882, and after due thought the two countries agreed in 1964 to build one. The tunnel is to be for railway stock only, so that no cars will be able to be driven through. The idea seems a little out-of-date before it starts.

Whenever the tunnel is actually built, it will only be the first in a series of links with Britain's nearer neighbours. This country lives by trade and it must be able to deliver goods as fast as other countries who have only to travel by land. Transport by sea is still a slow business. Suspension bridges have been suggested as alternative ways across the channel, in view of the fact that much experience of building long-span bridges is accumulating.

There is a further dimension to roads across the sea. Britain is getting short of land and of suitable places for storing drinking water. Many schemes have therefore been put forward to build dams across bays; some of the area inside is planned for reclamation, some for reservoirs and the dam becomes the base for a motorway. One such plan has been drawn up in detail for Morecambe Bay in Lancashire, another for the Bristol Channel. The time may come when dams are put across the English Channel and North Sea, adding much needed land to a crowded continent.

It is possible to get so immersed in science and in fantasy that the point of it is forgotten. The only reason for improving roads and designing vehicles is to make life richer for the people who use them. All the technical brilliance available will be of little use if it makes people the servants of machines. For example, many towns are preparing plans for complex internal motorways; but there will always be some people who cannot drive. They must not be forgotten in the plans, for the towns belong to them too. The cost of adapting towns to present-day needs so that all people are provided for is very high indeed. The loss to society if we exclude some kinds of people from development plans would be a far greater cost.

FURTHER READING

Books where some additional information can be found:
E. F. Carter, *Famous roads of the world*, Muller (1962); Charles S. Dunbar, *Buses, trolleys and trams*, Hamlyn (1967); S. E. Ellacott, *Wheels on the road*, Methuen Outlines series; ESA Information Book, *Roads, Motor cars;* Leonora Fry, *Bridges, Posts and telegraphs*, Methuen 'Get to know' series; D. Goldwater, *Bridges and how they are built*, The World's Work Ltd (1965); M. O. Greenwood, *Discovering roads and bridges*, ULP, 1964; M. Greenwood, *Roads and canals in the eighteenth century*, Longmans (1953); G. Hogg, *Blind Jack of Knaresborough*, Pheonix House (1967); D. B. Steinman and S. R. Watson, *Bridges and their builders*, Dover Publications Inc., New York (1957); P. Thornhill, *Roads and streets*, Methuen 'Get to know' series; R. J. Unstead, *Travel by road*, Black's junior reference books.

Books that deal with transport as a whole:
R. A. S. Hennessy, *Transport*, Batsford (1966); Jack Simmons, *Transport*, Studio Vista (1965); see also the maps drawn by the Ordnance Survey of Roman Britain and Britain in the Dark Ages.

Books that contain contemporary information:
There are pictures of roads or vehicles in the Picture Source Book series by Molly Harrison, Margaret Bryant and A. A. M. Wells, published by Allen and Unwin. J. Cadfryn-Roberts, *Coaches and trains*, The Ariel Press, London, has a number of nineteenth century engravings of stage coaches and roads, and J. M. Thomas, *Roads before the railways*, Evans, 1970, reproduces many documents. See also *The journeys of Celia Fiennes*, who travelled through parts of Britain at the end of the seventeenth century, edited by C. Morris, London (1947); Daniel Defoe, *A tour through the whole island of Great Britain*, Everyman's Library; Arthur Young, *Tour through the North of England*, 1770; and A. Bates, *Directory of stage coach services*, 1836, a modern compilation, published by David and Charles.

Most museums and libraries have maps made at different times. These are usually of towns before about 1750, but cover larger areas after that time. These are often hanging up for you to study, and copies can sometimes be bought. The ordnance survey maps began to be published in 1805 and the whole country was covered by 1873.

There are examples of road vehicles in many museums. A full list of the special collections is published each year in the guide called *Museums and Galleries*.

All documentary sources have to be treated with caution. Cartographers before the ordnance survey had few instruments and did not attempt to include every road. The writers tended to exaggerate, both in praise and condemnation. Nevertheless, they give first hand accounts of what the roads seemed like to them.

Books to dip into:

R. H. Cox, *The green roads of England*, Methuen (1934). (Deals with southern England only); I. D. Margary, *Roman roads in Britain*, John Baker (1967); E. Vale, *The mail-coach men*, David and Charles; L. T. C. Rolt, *Thomas Telford*; Samuel Smiles, *Lives of the engineers*, David and Charles.

Some local history societies and museums have produced booklets about roads in their own area. Ask for information at the library or museum.

Index

The numbers in **bold** type refer to the figure numbers of the illustrations.